Survival Guide for Coaching Youth Baseball

Dan Keller

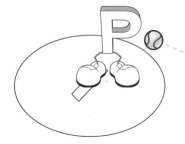

Human Kinetics

Library of Congress Cataloging-in-Publication Data

Keller, Dan (Daniel B.)
  Survival guide for coaching youth baseball / Dan Keller.
      p. cm.
  ISBN-13: 978-0-7360-8773-5 (soft cover)
  ISBN-10: 0-7360-8773-7 (soft cover)
  1. Baseball for children--Coaching. 2. Youth league baseball--Coaching. I.
Human Kinetics (Organization) II. Title.
  GV880.4.K45 2011
  796.357077--dc22
                                        2010039383

ISBN-10: 0-7360-8773-7 (print)
ISBN-13: 978-0-7360-8773-5 (print)

Copyright © 2011 by Human Kinetics, Inc.

Acquisitions Editor: Justin Klug; **Developmental Editor:** Kevin Matz; **Assistant Editors:** Steven Calderwood and Melissa J. Zavala; **Copyeditor:** Patrick Connolly; **Graphic Designer:** Nancy Rasmus; **Graphic Artist:** Julie L. Denzer; **Cover Designer:** Keith Blomberg; **Photographer (interior):** Neil Bernstein; **Visual Production Assistant:** Joyce Brumfield; **Photo Production Manager:** Jason Allen; **Art Manager:** Kelly Hendren; **Associate Art Manager:** Alan L. Wilborn; **Illustrator:** © Human Kinetics; **Printer:** Sheridan Books

We thank Le Bard Park in Huntington Beach, California, for providing the location for the photo shoot for this book.

Printed in the United States of America   10 · 9 8 7 6 5 4 3 2 1

The paper in this book is certified under a sustainable forestry program.

Human Kinetics
Web site: www.HumanKinetics.com

United States: Human Kinetics
P.O. Box 5076
Champaign, IL 61825-5076
800-747-4457
e-mail: humank@hkusa.com

Canada: Human Kinetics
475 Devonshire Road Unit 100
Windsor, ON N8Y 2L5
800-465-7301 (in Canada only)
e-mail: info@hkcanada.com

Europe: Human Kinetics
107 Bradford Road
Stanningley
Leeds LS28 6AT, United Kingdom
+44 (0) 113 255 5665
e-mail: hk@hkeurope.com

Australia: Human Kinetics
57A Price Avenue
Lower Mitcham, South Australia 5062
08 8372 0999
e-mail: info@hkaustralia.com

New Zealand: Human Kinetics
P.O. Box 80
Torrens Park, South Australia 5062
0800 222 062
e-mail: info@hknewzealand.com

E5001

Survival Guide for Coaching Youth Baseball

 Contents

Drill Finder

Drill title	Beginner	Intermediate	Advanced	Batting	Bunting	Throwing	Receiving	Fielding ground balls	Athleticism	Fielding fly balls	Pitching	Catching	Page no.
	Skill level			Skills									
Slow Rollers and Fundamentals	X						X	X					32
Dueling Fungoes		X						X					35
Box Drills	X					X	X	X					38
Ground Ball–Quick Catch	X						X	X	X				40
Double-Play Feeds		X				X		X					41
Thumbs Up, Pinkies Down	X						X						52
Four-Corners Receiving	X						X						54
Quarterback Tosses		X							X	X			57
Kick Back Jack		X					X						59
Tennis Racket Fly Balls			X							X			60
Broken Throwing	X					X							70
One-Knee Partner Catch	X					X							72
Sprint, Stop, Throw		X				X			X				74
Reaction Throwing	X					X			X				76
Five-Step Throwing Routine			X			X							78
Group Freeze Drills	X										X		94
Bullpen Buddies	X			X							X	X	96
Chair Drills		X									X		97
Homework—Individual Freeze Drills		X									X		100
Pitchers Fielding Practice (PFPs)			X					X			X		102
Three-Step Hitting	X			X									120
Tee Work With Stance and Grip	X			X									122
Getting Hit		X		X					X				125
Darts or Short Toss		X		X	X								127
Soft Toss With Details			X	X									129

 # Preface

The youth baseball coach is a mythical creature similar to a cross between Joe Torre and Kermit the Frog, Tommy Lasorda and Big Bird, or Sparky Anderson and Spongebob Squarepants! Equal parts team manager, sport psychologist, and sideshow entertainer, the job of a youth baseball coach can be both challenging and stressful. But, although there will be unavoidable struggles and unnecessary drama along the way, this fulfilling role can easily be the most rewarding coaching position of a parent's "career."

So . . . you find yourself standing and staring, clipboard in one hand, bucket of balls in the other. Your shirt's tucked in, sunglasses are on, and a shiny whistle hangs from your neck. But even though you look like Joe Torre, you're worried that you might manage more like Spongebob—especially considering that you can't stop these 12 rug rats from chasing the butterflies and that the majority of your first practice is spent teaching the group to make left-hand turns at every base.

Be not afraid! The *Survival Guide for Coaching Youth Baseball* is here. The daunting task of guiding a group of far-from-professional athletes through a season full of practices, games, and pizza parties just got a heck of a lot easier. This book is aimed at first-time coaches or parents who have chosen (or have been chosen) to lead a team of 5- to 10-year-old athletes. It provides an efficient and effective plan for teaching the game of baseball while developing solid fundamental skills and keeping kids entertained, engaged, and involved. With the help of this book, the first-time coach will be able to do the following:

- Establish team rules and guidelines for playing time, positions, and game competition.
- Evaluate players to determine realistic goals for development and training.
- Organize practices that maximize both fun and skill development.
- Create game plans that maximize enjoyment for athletes, coaches, and parents.
- Provide age-appropriate tips, and implement effective drills.
- Build a solid athletic fundamental base in the areas of hitting, pitching, and fielding.

- Educate kids on the benefit of teamwork, fair play, trying their hardest, and losing with dignity.
- Show young athletes why and how they can build character, strength, and integrity through competition and teamwork.

Making the commitment to coach youth baseball may or may not have been a well-thought-out decision. However, ensuring that the season is a successful one (defined by positive competition, athletic development, and maximum fun) most definitely can be. Coaching is an awesome opportunity to take a group of young athletes on the ride of their lives. The tips and strategies outlined in this book will help you plan a season full of terrific practices and fun games, so that everyone on board can have the best experience possible. Soon, you'll be known as the coach whom parents want their kids to play for. Those parents will know that your players get better and compete while having fun and learning to play the game the right way.

This book speaks to you in plain English. It's an easy read with clear-cut drill descriptions crafted to fit your age group. The following chapters highlight coaching and management techniques specific to running a youth team as well as provide guidance on teaching the fundamentals of baseball. And after you set down this book, you'll be armed with the knowledge to plan a practice in which players waste no time picking grass or digging holes.

This book is not about winning at all costs. Rather, winning becomes the by-product of putting a team in a position to maximize success and minimize the chance for injury. This is done with a balance of management skills and baseball knowledge—and a little bit of each goes a long way! Provided that you can keep the team learning and growing with smiles on their faces, winning will take care of itself, and the focus can remain on the development of your kids. This book embodies that philosophy and will be with you every step of the way. Read it once and then read it again. The *Survival Guide for Coaching Youth Baseball* is your guide to leading a group of individuals to a summer's worth of fun!

 Key to Diagrams

X — Any player

B — Batter

P — Pitcher

CA — Catcher

S — Shortstop

1 — First-base player

2 — Second-base player

3 — Third-base player

LF — Left fielder

CF — Center fielder

RF — Right fielder

C — Coach (or assistant coach or parent)

◉ — Baseball

△ — Cone

🪣 — Empty bucket

🪣 — Bucket of balls

 — Backstop/catchnet

——→ — Path of runner or fielder

----→ — Path of hit or throw

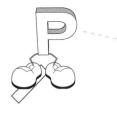

Help! Where Do I Start?

You've received your call-up . . . your cup of coffee . . . your opportunity to make it big as a baseball manager! But this is not the major leagues, with chartered jets, five-star hotels, and a roster full of the world's best players. Instead, your call-up came from the volunteer league board member letting you know that you've been "selected" to manage a local youth baseball team. Your cup of coffee came at the manager's meeting, where you listened to the rules and responsibilities of coaching, wondering why you ever got yourself into such a role. But with that behind you and the challenges of a season ahead of you, your opportunity to make it big is entirely real!

Never before have you had such an exciting opportunity to lead 12 young athletes through the time of their lives—they will be growing and learning, competing and complaining, succeeding and failing. Friendships will be forged, personalities shaped, and situations experienced that simply cannot be simulated away from the fields of competition. Coaching can be an exhilarating roller-coaster ride of character development and physical and mental improvement, with the chance to teach the fundamentals of a great game along the way.

A youth baseball coach can become entirely overwhelmed by the task of managing a team. After all, the coach must deal with the pressures of practices, games, and parents. And if you're a first-time coach, you may be facing a lot of pressure regarding topics that you know little about. Relax! If you can plan a single effective practice—which this book will assist you in doing—you can coach a team. It may seem intimidating now, but in four months you'll look back and laugh at how much fun you had. The show—maybe not "The Show"—but at least *a show* is about to begin!

Getting Started—Learning the Basics

Before the first practice, you need to have a basic understanding of baseball rules, field size and dimensions, and the minimum equipment necessary. Use the following information to prepare for early-season practices and to help plan the all-important preseason team meeting.

Know the Field

Baseball is "America's game," and the baseball field may be one of the most recognizable shapes on earth. From above, the field of play resembles an ice cream cone; home plate represents the bottom of the cone, and the outfield fence serves as the top of a well-rounded ice cream scoop. The baseball field has four bases, two batter's boxes, a pitcher's mound, and either 9 or 10 distinct positions:

1. Pitcher
2. Catcher
3. First base
4. Second base
5. Third base
6. Shortstop
7. Left field
8. Center field
9. Right field
10. Fourth outfielder (youngest levels)

Although most games will be played on a baseball field resembling figure 1.1, many practices will be held at city parks, neighborhood greenbelts, or school kickball areas. The field dimensions can vary wildly. Sometimes the field may include a pitching mound, backstop, and groomed infield. And other times, the field might be made up of a small patch of grass ridden with gopher holes and a line of bushes marking foul territory. Early in the season, you should find out where your squad

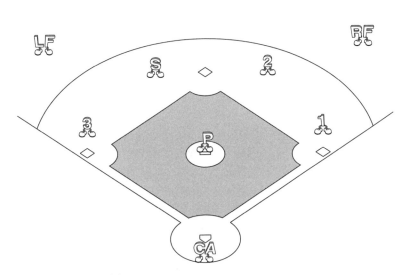

Figure 1.1   Fielder's positions.

will be practicing and exactly what the field dimensions and conditions are. Your practice plan will be directly related to the space, facilities, and equipment available.

Some leagues provide field space and specific times for your team to practice. In other leagues, the fields are allocated on a first-come, first-served basis. Sometimes coaches or parents will even volunteer to cut out of work early simply to get to the park and reserve a field (similar to the kid who left the lunch table early to ensure that he got the first game of tetherball). These communities have an unwritten rule rewarding the first person to be at a field in the afternoon. More strict leagues (often those that use fields on city parks) keep all teams OFF of the fields until game play begins. This is the toughest scenario, because the teams are sent scrambling to find field space on their own. In all cases, the search to find field space is a real issue but one that can be overcome with proper practice planning and space management. Find your practice area, map out the available and safe grounds, and get to work maximizing your time spent there.

Once your practice area is established, become familiar with the facilities. Are there restrooms available? Is there a safe area for athlete drop-off and pickup? Will you be able to use extra batting cages, bullpen areas, or even open grass for skill training or multiple stations? And just how much time will you have available on the field of play? This information will prove critical in mapping out and planning for a fun and busy practice with lots of movement and varying activities.

Coaching Equipment

Like that "golfer gadget guy," a baseball coach can quickly become inundated with the latest gimmicks and equipment designed to aid baseball performance. And although each of these fine pieces of technology likely has a time and place, most are not critical to the success of an eight-year-old. Here is a reasonable list of things to have with you when running a youth team:

- **Items that a coach should carry.** To run an effective workout, a coach should carry a clipboard (with the practice plan), a whistle, and a watch . . . and the coach should look darn good doing it. Sunglasses with reflective lenses, eye black, and tight elastic shorts are *not* necessary. However, a cell phone for emergency purposes is required and should be kept in a pocket or readily available nearby.

- **Gear bag.** Coaches of teams with players under seven years of age should use tennis balls or safety baseballs (soft stitch) to help avoid injuries as young kids learn to throw and catch. Small plastic disc cones, a batting tee, and a first aid kit can all be carried in a large gear bag. Most off-the-shelf first aid kits will work well, but be sure that the kit includes an instant cold pack, elastic bandages, Band-Aids, and CPR flashcards. Other recommended equipment includes Wiffle balls, a catch net (pop-up net for catching balls batted off a tee or from a soft toss), and an extra glove, bat, and helmet to accommodate those individuals in the rotating role of *forgetful kid* and *excuse-filled parent.*

- **Baseballs.** Simply put, the more baseballs you have, the easier your practice will be to run. The first-time coach will need to collect as many baseballs as possible. Whether they are safety or regular baseballs, the number of balls dictates the ability to break the team into smaller groups and run multiple drills at once. This allows assistant coaches to keep kids entertained, engaged, and having fun. Most coaches use buckets to gather and carry baseballs, and every coach should have a minimum of one full bucket that can be divided into at least two workout areas.

- **Coach's binder.** This administrative binder can be kept in your car or in the team gear bag. It should include emergency procedures as well as contact information and medical conditions (including allergies or health issues) for each player. The binder should also include any specific pickup or drop-off guidelines, birth certificates, league paperwork, and schedules (for practices, games, and snacks).

Player Equipment

Whether seeking equipment for your own kid or for the other 11 kids you are about to adopt, you can rest assured that a player only needs a minimal amount of gear in order to participate in a full practice. Most kids nowadays bring their own supplies to each event, including a helmet, bat, glove, and protective cup (never too early to protect one's manhood). Players usually carry these supplies in a baseball bag.

• **Player equipment bag.** Although any backpack or bag will do, baseball-specific athletic bags are available for purchase at sporting goods stores and can help to avoid lost equipment. These bags have a long pocket available to hold a bat, and they also have enough space to cram a helmet, cleats, and glove inside. Batting gloves are a nice option to include, and a baseball with family initials can make this bag ready for a big-league workout. Pack a bottle of water, and be sure to label everything with a last name and phone number. Kids may struggle to hit or pitch, but they usually excel at leaving their equipment behind! Teams will often be issued helmets, so be sure to ask about this before purchasing a helmet.

• **Player uniform.** At practice, athletes should wear baseball pants, a protective cup, and a hat. Some coaches like their athletes to wear a team T-shirt or other specifics, but this will vary. Athletes should bring a jacket and both cleats and athletic shoes. Here's a great tip to keep cars and homes clean: Instruct your athletes to arrive and leave in regular athletic shoes. They should keep their cleats inside the bag until they reach the ball field. At that time, the athletes take the cleats out of the bag, put them on, and put the athletic shoes in the bag. After practice, they reverse this procedure and put the normal athletic shoes on. Athletes should be sure to knock any dirt off of the cleats before jamming them into the bag. Your car will thank me later!

Know the Rules

The age of your players and the organization you participate with will determine many rules for competition. These include the distance between the bases, the distance from the pitching mound to home plate, and applicable rules or limitations related to playing time, positions played, and number of pitches thrown. At the youngest ages (4-6 years), tees will be used in place of any pitching. The next level up, typically 5 to 7 years of age, will involve coach pitching—something that is far more pressure packed than you might have imagined! The rules vary from league to league, but the adventure of kid-pitch baseball typically begins at age 7. Both basepath and pitching mound distances increase as the age of the athletes increases (table 1.1).

Table 1.1   Base Distance and Mound Distance for Various Ages

Age	Little League (bases / mound)	PONY League (bases / mound)	Travel Ball (bases / mound)
5	60 ft / NA	50 ft / NA	55 ft / NA
6	60 ft / NA	50 ft / NA	55 ft / NA
7	60 ft / 46 ft	55 ft / 38 ft	60 ft / NA
8	60 ft / 46 ft	55 ft / 38 ft	60 ft / 40 ft
9	60 ft / 46 ft	60 ft / 44 ft	65 ft / 44 ft
10	60 ft / 46 ft	60 ft / 44 ft	65 ft / 46 ft
11	60 ft / 46 ft	70 ft / 48 ft	70 ft / 50 ft
12	60 ft / 46 ft	70 ft / 48 ft	70 ft / 50 ft
13	90 ft / 60.5 ft	80 ft / 54 ft	80 ft / 54 ft
14	90 ft / 60.5 ft	80 ft / 54 ft	90 ft / 60.5 ft
15	90 ft / 60.5 ft	90 ft / 60.5 ft	90 ft / 60.5 ft
16	90 ft / 60.5 ft	90 ft / 60.5 ft	90 ft / 60.5 ft
17	90 ft / 60.5 ft	90 ft / 60.5 ft	90 ft / 60.5 ft
18	90 ft / 60.5 ft	90 ft / 60.5 ft	90 ft / 60.5 ft

Several major parent organizations are involved in youth baseball. Each organization plays under specific guidelines for field dimensions, playing time, and pitch counts. The organization associated with your league will issue specific bylaws and a rules handbook that you can study to determine what rules are applicable to the age group of your team.

Your local league will also follow rules on aspects such as game length, uniforms, and equipment allowed (e.g., bat regulations). Rules for game competition will include the strict or liberal interpretation of the strike zone, whether or not the teams will officially keep score (players are pretty skilled at determining who is winning regardless), and whether umpires will warn managers and athletes before enforcing other noncritical rules (balks, turning in after running through first base, and so on). You'll also need to delegate responsibility, or schedule your own time, to prep the field before play and after practice or games (cleanup crew).

Team Meetings and Communication

Your first task as a new manager is to hold a team meeting. This meeting is for both the players and their families, and it should be held off of the diamond at a team member's house (better start cleaning). The initial team meeting provides a chance to meet teammates and parents alike. At this meeting, you can break the ice and clearly communicate team goals as well as your own coaching philosophies.

The key to a smooth season as manager is honest and consistent communication. By agreeing to take this youth baseball team, you have signed on as a manager of people—youth and adult—and communication skills are an absolute necessity. This meeting is your first opportunity to establish the guidelines for the season ahead, to let parents know what will be expected of them, and to secure as much help as possible.

Team Meeting Highlights

Open the meeting by introducing yourself and each athlete and family. These are the players whom *you* scouted during tryouts and *you* selected during the draft. Get excited about your squad and pass that energy along to the families for the upcoming season. Share your own contact information and discuss important issues clearly and quickly—no one likes a yawner. Here are some issues that should be discussed:

- **Emergency information.** Protect yourself and your players. Collect vital information from parents by having them fill out a medical card (most leagues provide standardized and organization-mandated cards). Ideally, you should be CPR trained, carry a cell phone at all times, and have emergency supplies and procedures on hand. Make sure the forms include an area where parents can provide their own contact information and can share any sensitive information or other requests.

- **Schedules.** Parents appreciate early notice so that they can plan around your practices. Before the initial team meeting, you should finalize the practice schedule leading up to the first week of games. You can always switch days or times if necessary, but doing this early will help with practice attendance and allow for consistent development. Clearly communicate your expectations regarding punctuality and attendance—it is appropriate to expect everyone else's commitment to match your own.

- **Practices.** Practices should be scheduled on regular days and times, and you should complete the practice schedule as early in advance as possible. Parents appreciate this because many schedule their lives around their children's activities.
- **Games.** The game schedule will be provided by the league, but you can establish a regular regimen for the pregame, including the arrival time (45-60 minutes before game time).
- **Snacks.** Quite possibly the most important schedule of all, the snack schedule should rotate the responsibility for bringing snacks among the parents. Publish the schedule at the team meeting and allow parents to switch if necessary. Communicate how important snacks are and keep a backup (nonperishable) snack supply in your car—you don't want to have a snackless squad of soldiers.

Get Help: Involve Parents

There is a distinct difference between managing a team and serving in the role of coach. You've taken on the manager position and volunteered to schedule practices and lead the team. Therefore, you will need as much help as possible. You'll need assistant coaches, a team mom, and a Web site or communications officer. You'll also need some game volunteers to keep score, count pitches, clean the field, and handle other responsibilities. The league will undoubtedly assign several roles that you must find people to fill. Many coaches struggle to do this. Use the team meeting to fill these roles—do not leave this meeting without filling each league responsibility and volunteer role!

You should select two or three able and willing assistant coaches. These coaches will be in uniform for games and will assist with practices. Enlist as many additional volunteers as possible to also help with practices and team functions. The more the merrier—delegate your heart out! You've made the most difficult commitment; you're in charge, but you're going to need help. The team meeting is your best chance of securing helpers.

Coaching Philosophy—Define, Establish, and Communicate

For this final part of the team meeting, you may want to send the kids into the garage to play table tennis or out into the yard to play Wiffle ball. Take this opportunity to clearly communicate your coaching philosophy—something that you'll have to take some time to think through before the meeting. Sharing your philosophy with the parents will help you avoid issues down the road. Unfortunately, competition coupled with egos will undoubtedly bring out the worst in many parents. If you clearly communicate your philosophy and big-picture perspective at the team meeting, the critical decisions during the season will be much easier for you to make and much easier for other parents to understand.

Coaching youth baseball is a delicate balance of playing to win versus playing to develop. The chance of a high school athlete playing some form of professional baseball is .5 percent (and even more slim when it comes to playing in the big leagues). For a youth baseball player, making the high school squad has grown increasingly competitive as well. At an average high school, seven athletes in each graduating class will letter on the varsity baseball team. This means that the majority of your youth players will not play high school baseball, let alone in college or professionally.

Develop and define your role as a youth baseball coach: You are a teacher of the fundamentals of the game, a provider of opportunities for athletes to perform and succeed, and the captain of a ship that will zig and zag but eventually reach the end-of-season port. Practices and games should blend fun with competition. Make sure your athletes smile regularly. Remind them that at its core, baseball is a *game* and must remain one. Your athletes will learn valuable life lessons and will endure pressures and stresses, but this game is supposed to be fun. At times, you should do something silly and funny to break the tension. Cut a practice short and play over-the-line, do relay races as a warm-up, or finish practice with a sunflower seed spitting contest. Stay positive and emphasize what you *do* want done—not what you *don't* want done. Good sporting behavior is key, and respect for everyone builds a true champion. Say it, mean it, and write it down . . . you will be tested. When developing your coaching philosophy, you should also address each of these points:

- **Team goals.** Your goal is consistent improvement. Practices are for coaches; games are for the players. This means that practices will be the opportunity for coaches to help athletes work on fundamental skills. Games will then be the chance for athletes to play—with aggression and confidence and without fear of failure. Over the course of the season, athletes should physically improve and mentally work to avoid making the same mistakes over and over.

- **Playing time.** Many leagues dictate minimum innings played, which will provide a starting point for playing time. All athletes should sit out at some point each game, and playing time should be allocated equally at the youngest levels. If you establish a clear formula for playing time, the emotion of making decisions about playing time is removed, and all parents know where their athletes stand. Even with equal playing time, a team can still compete by playing its more skilled players at important positions during the early and late innings.

• **Positions.** Athletes should rotate between positions. As athletes grow older, the number of positions played will decrease, and the number of innings spent at one or two positions will increase. For beginning baseball, all athletes should spend time both in the infield and the outfield. Safety must be taken into account, keeping in mind that first base, pitcher, and catcher are the most difficult positions to fill. Find ways to let as many interested athletes play these positions as possible. If an athlete wants to pitch, find the situation where he can pitch—whether it's when you're down by 10 or up by 10, there *will* be a time to get him onto the mound.

• **Homework.** A big part of consistent improvement in young athletes is parent support and buy-in. Communicate the importance of the parents' support in their children's development as baseball players. You should assign regular homework to the players, and the parents need to follow up to ensure that the players get the necessary work off of the field.

• **Attendance and punctuality.** You might not be able to avoid having late players or other attendance-related issues. However, you need to find a way to drive home the message that commitment is key, practice makes perfect, and punctuality at all functions is a sign of respect for the volunteers donating hours of their time. Include guidelines for what to wear and bring to practices, proper attire (baseball pants, protective cup), and supplies (water, glove, hat).

• **Communication.** Address appropriate communication procedures for all people who are a part of this team:

  • Coaches should remain positive, avoid profanity, and lead by example.

  • Parents should avoid coaching from the stands, berating umpires, or negatively engaging any members of the opposing team or their parents. Request that parents approach you and address any issues away from the field and the athletes. Provide days and times that you can be reached to discuss anything related to the team.

  • Athletes should not argue with umpires, and they should not taunt or disrespect their opponents. Respect and positive sporting behavior should be shown to umpires, opposing teams, and their parents.

The Coach's Clipboard

✔ Get familiar with the traditional baseball field and the unique surroundings of your own practice site.

✔ Prepare for emergencies with medical cards and player information.

✔ Bring a gear bag containing balls, cones, a glove, and a first aid kit.

✔ Baseballs, baseballs, baseballs—obtain as many as you can get your hands on!

✔ Study league rules and age-specific guidelines (distances, playing time, positions, and so on).

✔ Host a team meeting where you collect information, establish team rules, and get help.

✔ Define your own coaching philosophy focused on player development and good sporting behavior, and clearly communicate the season's goals to parents and athletes.

✔ Smile, take a deep breath, and jump in!

Organizing Your Team

With your initial research and development concluded, you are now ready to dive into the nuts and bolts of coaching baseball. You've got your bases covered (literally), your equipment bag feels as if two players are riding inside it, and a field practice site is locked down and reserved. You now understand that a strike is a good thing, an error not so good, and the team making the most left turns on the bases wins. Also, you've had (and probably hosted) a team meeting to meet and greet the families, to establish team guidelines and expectations, and to communicate your coaching philosophy. It's time to get this team onto the field!

Management 101

The art of managing a youth baseball team is very similar to running a small business unit. The process involves big-picture goals and plans, with a series of individual tasks or projects taking place along the way. Toss in 2 or 3 coaches to manage and 10 to 12 worker bees to direct, and this process can quickly become daunting. The information in this section will help alleviate any overwhelming feelings you may be having about your role as a beginning baseball coach. The best way to do this is to break down the responsibilities of a manager into a series of simple, manageable tasks.

In Management 101, the first step is to clearly define the different roles of *manager* and *coach,* keeping in mind that you will undoubtedly be filling both roles. The manager assumes responsibility for mapping out the top-level snapshot (season plan) and then all the projects along the way (practice plans). The majority of a manager's work takes place away from the field of play, and this allows a coach's activities to remain on the field. A coach's responsibility begins once the players arrive and the practice or game begins. However, the activities involved during this time are directly tied to the plan laid out by the manager. Coaches coach—that's what they volunteered for and what you need to empower them to do. Spend 60 minutes researching and mapping out your season's goals; then spend a half hour a week to lay out a practice plan. If you do this, your volunteer assistants will show up to the field prepared and excited to coach. Perhaps more important, so will you! As mentioned, the head coach serves in the role of both manager and coach. By respecting the role of manager, you give yourself the opportunity to coach once practice begins.

Finally, proper team management allows each volunteer to coach to the best of his or her own abilities, whatever those abilities may be. You do not have to be an expert to coach baseball! With a well-thought-out practice plan, everyone involved—most important, the athletes—will experience the most fun and fulfillment possible. Ultimately, that is why you, the assistant coaches, and the participating families have signed up to be a part of this baseball team. Effective team management helps ensure that the time spent on the field is productive and fun. Invest in Management 101 and everyone wins!

Structure, Structure, Structure

A discussion on coaching youth baseball will eventually revert back to structure. Any group of people needs structure and guidance to function efficiently. And when that group of people is made up of five- and six-year-olds, the concept of structure and guidance becomes infinitely more important! The following sections lay out the planning areas needed when starting a team: season planning, practice planning, and game planning. Follow this guide and take the time to script a season plan as well as the first team practice plan. From there, coaches can coach, players can play, and our discussion moves on to the fun stuff—balls and bats, throwing and hitting. Note: You should follow these guides and create electronic documents for each section. Templates for each document are available online at www.lifeletics.com. If you end up enjoying the experience of coaching, your subsequent seasons will be dramatically easier if you already have a working season plan and a pocket full of practice plans.

Season Planning In a nutshell, season planning entails laying out (in a single document) all that you want to cover in a baseball season. What are the main skills, fundamentals, and areas of instruction that you want to cover over the course of the four months spent with this team? And how can you effectively list them to make sure that you are responsibly teaching what these athletes need? From this season plan document, you will pull several of these topics into each specific practice plan. All topics should eventually be covered at some point during the season.

The season plan document should include two columns for "dates covered." A reasonable goal is to cover each line item twice. Depending on your group of athletes, you will likely cover certain specifics three, four, or even five times. Laugh and chuckle, this *is* the joy of youth coaching. Using this list and your own additions—and keeping in mind your level of play—begin the season plan by prioritizing those areas that you want to practice before the first game. Suggested topics include team defense basics, hitting and fielding fundamentals, and perhaps even a session about which hand to wear the glove on, how to blow a bubble, or how to spit sunflower seeds. These are the items to highlight for your first five or six practices.

As previously stated, the one-page season plan lays out the main subject areas of baseball, along with the specific fundamentals falling within each subject area. The season plan should be clean and thorough, and it should allow room to note when each area will be covered in practice. Figure 2.1 on page 16 shows a sample season plan for the beginning baseball coach.

Practice Planning Practice planning is the most important responsibility of the head coach (or manager) in youth baseball, and it will make or break your season. By planning your practices well, you'll be able to offer fun and efficient practices, and the athletes, parents, and coaches will all have a great experience. If you don't plan your practices effectively, the dreaded "youth sports drama monster" will grow frustrated and angry—kids will get bored, coaches will become frustrated, and parents will whisper. You'll quickly wonder why you ever signed up to coach.

To ensure that no monsters climb out of the stands, take 10 minutes before practice to lay out the day's itinerary (including drills and associated times). Try to maximize limited time and field space. Use the information included in the season plan as your guide to effectively schedule each practice using a standard practice plan document (see the sample in figure 2.2, p. 17). Break each practice down into designated time blocks, and assign a relevant drill or task to each time block. This ensures that the coaches have a chance to plan out their own stations and that the athletes are occupied, engaged, and having fun.

Figure 2.1   Sample Season Plan

Dates Covered		Category
		Team Defense
		Basics: positions, throw ball around IF, taking the field
		Ground ball repetitions
		Fly ball repetitions
		Rundowns
		Cuts and relays
		Bunt defense
		1/3 defense
		Pick-offs
		Pregame routine
		PFP's (pitcher fundamental practice)
		Situations: rotations and responsibilities
		Bullpens
		Baseball athleticism training
		Individual Defense
		Infield: ground ball fundies
		Outfield: fly ball fundies
		Position specific training (catcher, pitcher, etc.)
		Baseball athleticism training
		Team Offense
		Batting practice: repetitions
		Batting practice: live
		Batting practice: cage work
		Bunting
		Baserunning: leads and breaks, bases
		Scrimmage and intrasquad
		1/3 offense
		Offensive situations and execution
		Individual Offense
		Swing training (breakdown as appropriate)
		Execution: slash, right side, off-speed
		Bunt training: sac, push, drag, squeeze
		Stealing bases
		Team
		Signs
		Dugout etiquette
		Practice structure schedule
		Game structure schedule
		Communication: rules, attire, etc.
		Practice Absolutes
		Run, stretch, and throw
		Long toss
		Conditioning
		Pitchers' bullpens

From D. Keller, 2011, *Survival Guide for Coaching Youth Baseball* (Champaign, IL: Human Kinetics).

Figure 2.2   Sample Defensive Practice Plan

Date: Thursday, 2/15, 3:30 p.m.
Field: Field #3

Start Time	End Time	Activity or Drill
3:30	3:45	Run, stretch, and throw

3:45	4:15	Team defense:
		  Bunt defense
		  1/3 defense

4:15	**4:20**	**Water Break**

4:20	4:45	Individual defense:
		Station instruction work
		  Infield: Ground ball fundies
		  Outfield: Fly ball fundies
		  All: Cuts and relays

4:45	5:10	Team defense:
		  Basics: Positions and infield throws
		  Ground ball repetitions: Dueling fungoes
		  Fly ball repetitions
		  Pregame routine

From D. Keller, 2011, *Survival Guide for Coaching Youth Baseball* (Champaign, IL: Human Kinetics).

Two main topics are associated with the practice plan:

1. Time blocks: Divide each practice into several time blocks of 10 to 30 minutes.
2. Station instruction: Involve multiple areas of activity during each time block of instruction.

For each specific practice plan, divide the available time into several time blocks of 10 to 30 minutes. Each of these time blocks will then involve multiple stations of instruction depending on how many coaches are available. If you have two assistant coaches and yourself, then each time block can involve as many as three stations. Each station, in turn, will involve a specific area of baseball instruction—as pulled from the season plan.

The importance of station instruction (or work areas) lies in the ability to minimize the number of athletes in each group and maximize the amount of instruction offered during each practice. If three coaches are available—and therefore three stations—a typical team of 12 athletes can be broken down into 3 groups of 4. This results in more individual attention and instruction for each athlete, and it provides a better coaching environment for the volunteer coach. The lower numbers help prevent kids from standing in lines or waiting around, decreasing the chances for distractions or horsing around.

Use the main categories from the season plan to select a baseball category for each time block. For example, let's use team defense as our selected category for the first time block (TB1). Because you have two assistant coaches helping with practice, you can set up three stations to be used during TB1 (and each of the other time blocks). Select three specific topics from the team defense category to cover at these stations (at three separate areas on the field). On the main diamond, one coach could walk through the positions on the field and describe how the team will sprint to their positions each inning (beginning basics). Down the left-field line, another coach could explain the proper fundamentals for executing cuts and relays, which may quickly turn into more of a discussion about catching and throwing. A third coach could set up in the area of the right-field line; this coach could hit ground balls and discuss fielding technique (ground-ball instruction). See figure 2.2 for a more detailed example of how to schedule a practice.

Effective planning is absolutely necessary for a smooth practice or game. If you can send the practice plan or game plan to your assistant coaches an hour or two before the event, you will give them the chance to come up with a plan for each of their stations. Doing this is important because it means that any volunteer coach does not have to be an expert. When the coaches know what their responsibility will be for each practice, they can call a friend, go online, or consult a book to find a couple fun drills.

Game Planning
Planning for game day is much easier than planning for a practice. Basically, you'll have pregame, in-game, and postgame responsibilities. Typically, teams are required to arrive 45 minutes to an hour before game time. And although you may end up using 30 of those minutes to check for lost gloves, to find that elusive belt loop, or to corral all 12 kids inside the dugout, the game plan is a document designed to organize what both the athletes and the coaches are doing. Coaches need to prep the field and stands for game play, chalk the lines and batter's box, retrieve scoreboard and snack bar equipment, and warm up the athletes.

The example in figure 2.3 specifically designates a block for team time. This important 10 to 15 minutes can be used to address any team issues or topics requiring discussion. Review missed signs, highlight broken rules (such as no sunflower seeds), or discuss team goals for the day's game. Team time can switch to baseball-related warm-up drills if nothing needs to be said in a meeting.

Figure 2.3   Sample Game Plan

Date: Saturday, 2/24, 11:00 a.m.
Field: Field #2

Start Time	End Time	Activity
10:00	10:20	Athletes dressed, ready promptly at 10:00 a.m. Run, stretch, and throw.
10:20	10:35	Team time: Pepper games, BP, GBs, and FBs Announcements: signs, plays Team meeting
10:35	10:45	Pregame
10:45	10:50	Team sprints: Right field line Leads and breaks
10:50	11:00	Pitcher warm-up Starting pitcher to bullpen Umpire meeting
11:00	12:30	Game time! Postgame: Right field line Meeting: needs discussion, week ahead

From D. Keller, 2011, *Survival Guide for Coaching Youth Baseball* (Champaign, IL: Human Kinetics).

A final component of the game plan is to delegate game-day responsibilities. During pregame, the responsibilities include field prep, athlete warm-up, and coaching duties (equipment, dugouts, and lineups). Game time brings forth defensive positioning, offensive base coaching, and dugout patrol. Postgame responsibilities include field cleanup, equipment breakdown, and the team speech.

Remember that planning can never prepare you for what is to come during a game. It's often said that practices are for the coaches, and games are for the players. Do your best to enjoy kids being kids. Butterflies *are* intriguing, the dirt is fun to play with, and third base looks an awful lot like first base! This is their time to shine, their moment for glory, and their opportunity to *play*.

Management 101 Tips

Here are some basic tips for running practices. Keep these in mind and you'll be sure to have successful and fun practices.

- **Make practices efficient and fun.** It is said that a good practice is one where the athletes had fun—but a great practice is one where the athletes also improved. Therefore, your goal is to produce a practice where efficiency, competition, and instruction come together to keep things moving quickly for the athletes. Mask the instruction (or the work) with games, points, and prizes. Get creative and innovative, and involve positive competition whenever possible to keep athletes engaged, entertained, and occupied.

- **Discuss, show, go.** Kids learn in different ways. For each skill or drill, you'll want to first describe the drill (athletes hear). Then, look for a volunteer or select an athlete who knows how to do this movement and have him show the group (athletes see). Finally, get out of the way and let the kids play (athletes feel)! Learning happens by doing—not watching.

- **Teach players to have no fear of failure.** To learn, athletes cannot fear failure. It's an old but true cliche: Baseball is a game of failure. Hitters will strike out, pitchers will give up home runs, and fielders will make errors. Although we don't want to celebrate these errors, as baseball coaches we must realize that *this* is how athletes learn. Baseball is a powerful teacher, and failure allows athletes to grow both as competitors and as young people. Along the way, these young athletes must not be afraid to swing, throw, or field with full effort. Help the athletes learn from their mistakes; don't berate them and make them scared to succeed.

- **Run, stretch, and then throw.** Before any athlete is allowed to touch a baseball, the team should first run and then stretch. Running gets the blood flowing, and stretching prepares the muscles to work. Although it is true that young athletes are resilient, you should establish a mandatory rule of running then stretching then throwing in order to help them build healthy and safe habits. Start each practice and game with the sequence of run, stretch, throw.

- **Include conditioning (but call it baserunning).** Just as you should start practice with run–stretch–throw, you should be sure to finish practice with conditioning. Creative practice planning can mask the negative aspects of conditioning by combining it with baserunning fundamentals, relay races, or agility movements.

- **Keep a practice log.** Keep a concise list of the stations covered at each practice. You've already got a season plan, and you will compile a season's worth of practice plans. To have an idea of what's been covered and how long it's been since a specific drill has been run, you should keep a log of the stations offered at each practice.

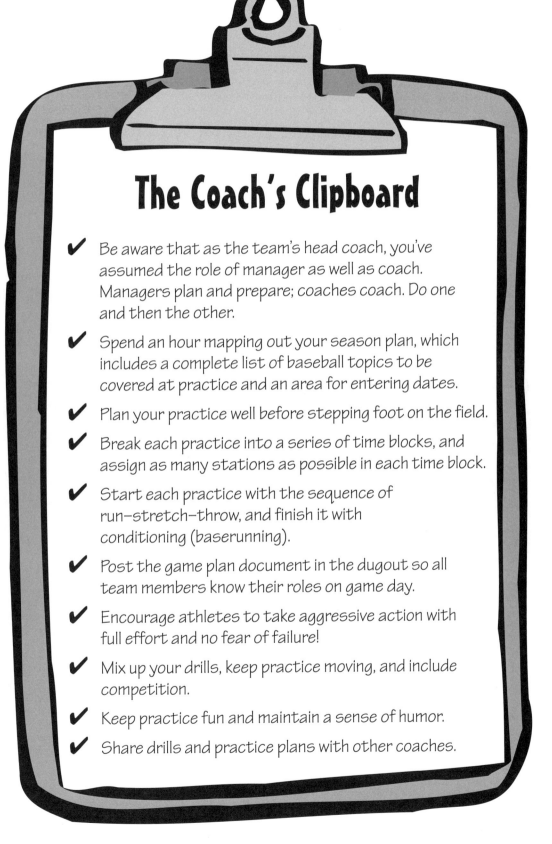

The Coach's Clipboard

✔ Be aware that as the team's head coach, you've assumed the role of manager as well as coach. Managers plan and prepare; coaches coach. Do one and then the other.

✔ Spend an hour mapping out your season plan, which includes a complete list of baseball topics to be covered at practice and an area for entering dates.

✔ Plan your practice well before stepping foot on the field.

✔ Break each practice into a series of time blocks, and assign as many stations as possible in each time block.

✔ Start each practice with the sequence of run–stretch–throw, and finish it with conditioning (baserunning).

✔ Post the game plan document in the dugout so all team members know their roles on game day.

✔ Encourage athletes to take aggressive action with full effort and no fear of failure!

✔ Mix up your drills, keep practice moving, and include competition.

✔ Keep practice fun and maintain a sense of humor.

✔ Share drills and practice plans with other coaches.

Developing Fielding Skills With 5 Simple Drills

As discussion moves into baseball fundamentals, you need to understand that there is a huge difference between *executing* a specific movement and *teaching* the movement. This chapter, for example, first addresses the fundamentals associated with fielding a ground ball. Information about teaching athletes to field ground balls is covered second. With beginning fielders, you should teach a series of basic steps that will place the athlete in an optimal position to make a play. Beyond that, the varying athletic abilities of each individual will dictate how deeply you dive into the fundamentals of fielding.

Fielding 101

The life of a baseball coach would be much less difficult if athletes could simply do what they're told: "Charge the ball, pick it up, and throw it to first base!" In theory, fielding a ground ball is a simple movement. After all, you've watched major leaguers on TV do it for years . . . and they make it look so easy. In reality, catching a bouncing, spinning, and moving ball cleanly and quickly can be very difficult. Making an accurate throw after fielding said ground ball and doing all of this with the added pressure of a runner barreling down the line can make this one of the most difficult plays in baseball.

To properly field a ground ball, a player needs to perform four distinct movements:

1. Ready position
2. Approach
3. Fielding triangle
4. Pop, shuffle, and throw

Ready Position

The ready position (figure 3.1) for an infielder is an athletic stance that ensures the infielder is paying attention and places him in the optimal fielding position to attack a ground ball. Physically, the athlete's weight is centered on the balls of the feet, and the knees are slightly bent; the arms are hanging loosely beside the body, and the palms of the hands are turned open (facing home plate). When teaching the ready position, use a cone to help show players how to center their weight. Athletes should move into the ready position just before each pitch is released—this is something that will take plenty of practice and a bucket full of reminders. The real goal of teaching a ready position is to have all athletes ready to move on contact. A good team motto is "20 eyes on home plate!" Set a team goal of having 18 or 20 eyeballs looking at home plate when the opposing batter gets ready to swing.

More technically, a proper ready position ensures that when a ground ball is hit, the athlete's first step can be right or left as necessary. This athletic and balanced position helps accomplish this by limiting any movement forward at contact. By limiting any forward movement, the athlete can maximize his range (the lat-

Figure 3.1   The ready position.

eral distance he can cover to field ground balls) and thus the number of grounders reached. If the feet are moving toward home plate at delivery, the athlete will not be ready to move laterally on contact.

To help your athletes get into the fielding position, Lifeletics recommends that you teach a "right, left, hop" movement. This ensures that at the time the pitcher delivers the baseball, the fielder has hopped into a ready position (weight is evenly distributed between the balls of the feet, hands are open, and knees are bent). Just before a pitch is released, every player should take a step with the right foot, followed by a step with the left foot, and then finish with a small hop into the ready position. Use a fun description such as "shake the earth," or coin a phrase such as the "gorilla stomp." You can even allow the players to name their own ready position hop.

Approach

Once the ball is hit, the fielder must approach the baseball in an effort to most efficiently and effectively field the ground ball cleanly and be in a position to make an accurate throw. This is commonly referred to as "charging the baseball" (and is really nothing more than that for beginning baseball players). Without rushing, or overrunning the baseball, novice fielders should simply move in the direction of the ground ball in an effort to shorten the time it takes to get the ball to first base.

To teach proper approach, use a technique I call the *banana curve.* The banana curve is most easily described on a ground ball hit directly at a fielder. A more advanced fielder will use this technique to surround the baseball so that his momentum is moving toward first base. From a shortstop's perspective, this means that a fielder will move to his right slightly while charging the ground ball to get a good hop. This movement takes the path of a curved banana (figure 3.2), much

Figure 3.2   The banana curve.

like the direction taken when rounding first base on a single. Use cones as a physical guide to teach the surrounding path of a proper approach.

Fielding Triangle

Get down early and be athletic! After the fielder recognizes the ball off the bat and takes some sort of approach toward the baseball, it's now time to field that sucker. Athletes should get in front of every ground ball possible and should assume the fielding triangle position. Simply put, the fielding triangle (figure 3.3) gives a young fielder the best chance for success—it gives the hands space to reach out and receive the ball, and it allows the hips to move and adjust athletically. The triangle position also gets the fielder's eyes down low (closer to the baseball's bounding path) and puts the feet in position to easily move after receiving the baseball.

Figure 3.3 The fielding triangle.

The fielding position referred to as a triangle is actually shaped by the position of the right foot, the left foot, and the hands. These three body parts end up in a triangular shape, with the hands well in front of the body and positioned at the top or peak of the triangle. The back of the glove touches the ground, with the palm facing forward, while the off hand hovers directly above the glove. This forms the all-important "alligator mouth," which will be used to clamp down and devour the baseball once in the glove. You should introduce the triangle position very early in the practice schedule. This position should be coached and trained regularly and should be encouraged throughout the entire season. Here are the key points regarding this position:

- Feet are spread beyond shoulder-width apart.
- Knees are bent, and the butt is down—sitting in a chair.
- Hands are out—the throwing hand is open and above the glove (alligator mouth).
- Head is down—the button of the cap should tilt forward.

You want to teach kids to get down early. It's very common for beginning baseball players to overrun ground balls. Judging speed and distance is something that must be learned over years and years of play. Encourage athletes to get to the fielding position early and allow this process to take place. Much like taking a step and loading the hands before a hitter's swing, an infielder must be in the fielding triangle before attempting to field a ground ball. Getting down early and receiving the baseball will keep the feet out of the way and allow the hands to have the opportunity to move in front of the body. This gives the fielder time and space to adjust for bad hops. Over time, the fielder will develop a positive habit of getting down early!

Pop, Shuffle, Throw

Provided the ball has found its way into the athlete's glove, the fielder now needs to finish the play with a strong and accurate throw. Affectionately referred to as "pop, shuffle, throw," the movement after fielding the ball helps the athlete to gain momentum and direct it toward the target. Simply put, the athlete needs to get his body moving toward the target before making a throw.

Pop   The first movement of this process is a step with the throwing-arm foot in the direction of the target. For a right-handed shortstop, this would be a direct step toward first base with the right foot and the beginning movement to generate momentum. The right foot moves in front of the left foot (crossover step) (figure 3.4a), with the inside of the ankle pointing directly toward the target. Next, the left foot steps toward the target helping to turn the body sideways (front shoulder and hip pointing toward the target) in preparation for the throw.

During this step, the hands separate, the glove reaches out toward first base, and the hand takes the ball back behind the athlete's head. As with all beginning baseball techniques, you should teach the feet first. Drill the back-foot step in front of the front foot before worrying about the hands separating. At Lifeletics, we drill separation after establishing footwork. Athletes are instructed to consciously separate before moving out of the fielding triangle position. The faster the ball gets into the throwing hand, the sooner the hands and feet are athletically moving together. This brings the baseball into proper throwing position and allows for an accurate throw. At its most basic, this movement can be performed by trying to cross the back foot over as the hands separate. In a more advanced rhythm, the athlete's movement would be as follows: field, separate, step, and then shuffle and throw!

Shuffle   Now it's time to generate some power! If not taught to take a shuffle, athletes will field the ball, spin on their back foot, and unleash a rainbow in the vicinity of first base. Provided the baseball does not draw rain, the chances of it coming down somewhere near the bag are about 50-50. To combat this lollipop throw, the player's next step in fielding a ground ball should be to perform a shuffle movement with the feet. This shuffle step is an athletic movement designed to build power and energy into the throw, and it can be taught as *clicking your heels* or *side skipping* toward first base (figure 3.4b). The player should field the ground ball, step with the back foot, follow with the front foot, and then take an aggressive shuffle (or two).

Throw   After executing a proper fielding triangle, separating the hands, and shuffling the feet, the athlete should be in a strong throwing position. The athlete's arms should be extended, the feet spread, and the weight loaded on the back leg (figure 3.4c). As a rule, you should teach athletes to maintain a hand position on top of the baseball, avoiding any sidearm throws. As a coach, if you've guided the athlete's movements correctly to this position, the rest is up to him. All you can do now is cross your fingers and hope for the best.

Figure 3.4   *(a)* Pop, *(b)* shuffle, and *(c)* throw.

Teaching Infielders

Understanding how to field a ground ball is entirely different than teaching infielders how to do it. To teach the actions of proper ground-ball technique, you need to use a structured plan over several practices—and you must have plenty of patience. Begin by using slow rollers from the hand (no batted balls), and focus your instruction on footwork. Over time, break down the fundamental steps, giving the athletes time to understand and execute the various movements before you increase the pace and ultimately hit ground balls.

Note that there is a time for teaching and a time for repetitions. In this case, this means that you may not hit ground balls off the bat when you are working on *instruction.* However, kids also need to field ground balls, even if their technique isn't perfect. They need the practice, and they need to learn about long hops, short hops, different spins, and so on. This helps ensure that the kids are having fun (all work and no play makes a grumpy ballplayer), and it enables them to gain invaluable real-life experience by having a ball go through their legs, off of their chest, or in and out of their glove.

Order of Instruction

Before covering specific fielding drills, you need to understand the proper order of instruction. Although it is important to make sure that all material is covered, your main goal is helping the athletes improve. By understanding the order of operation, you can drastically increase the collective level

Beginning Terms and Tips

- **Athlete listening position**—Shoulder to shoulder facing the coach.
- **Right, left, throw**—Footwork after fielding the ground ball (insert *shuffle* before *throw* if appropriate).
- **Ankle eye**—Inside ankle of the crossover foot; points to the target.
- **Point glove and throw**—Basic instruction for throwing.
- **Alligator hands**—Position of the hands at the fielding triangle.
- **Momentum shuffles**—Executed after fielding and stepping, but before throwing.

of retention and increase the team's chance of successful learning. This coaching process will take place over the course of several practices, a number of drills, and a variety of exercises. However, a station dedicated to only teaching is necessary before and during all the practice drills. Here is the suggested order of instruction for effective coaching:

1. **Slow rollers.** Underhand slow rollers while providing little instruction. Establish a relaxed pace so that the athletes are not rushing, and observe tendencies and habits. In the instruction process, you will next break down each part of the fielding motion before returning to working on a full ground ball.

2. **Fielding triangle.** Discuss the fundamentals needed to properly field a ground ball. Explain body positioning and the fact that this position helps the fielder receive a good hop (no bobbles).

3. **Execution rollers.** Provide slow rollers and focus on teaching the fielding triangle, the correct separation of the hands, and an aggressive shuffle along with a throw to a target. Start slow and increase the pace. Insert pauses or freezes at some of the positions to make sure the athletes feel their body moving through the phases of fielding a ground ball correctly.

4. **Ready position and approach.** Describe the big picture and put the ground-ball process together: "What happens before the ball is actually in your glove?" The ready position allows an athlete to get a good break on the ball, and a banana curve approach ensures that the body is in front of the ball and in a proper fielding triangle. Momentum will be gathered toward the target with a subtle curve around the baseball.

5. **Batted balls.** Now athletes are ready to receive ground balls off of the bat. Instruct the athletes to get into ready position when the ball is tossed up. Next, they execute the approach, field, and throw.

Keep your energy high and your instruction simple, focusing on footwork and fundamentals first. The pace of instruction should be slow enough that the athletes stay under control and experience the act of fielding ground balls correctly. Create an atmosphere where the athletes do not rush their hands and feet. Drill athleticism first, and speed up the pace as improvements are seen. Once the athletes are able to execute consistently, you should apply drills that will focus on these movements.

Be Aggressive!

Infielders should be encouraged to be aggressive and not fear failure. Errors are a part of the game, and an athlete must know that he is free to make an aggressive movement and throw without being yelled at. Coaches need to understand the difference between physical and mental errors, and they should focus more on correcting the mental errors. Train infielders from the ground up, focusing on clean and controlled footwork at a smooth pace. Increase speed, difficulty, and intensity as appropriate.

Five Minutes for Fielding

When you are using the practice-planning methods described in chapter 2, the fielding portion of a practice can start immediately after playing catch. After a good throwing session, the athletes are in perfect position to work on a fielding drill (ground ball or quick catch, box drills, or even basic receiving). For younger age groups, the athletes can break into small groups to work on simple throwing or receiving drills using tennis balls or soft baseballs. Whether this takes 5 minutes or 50 minutes, the time between throwing and taking the field can be very productive.

Drill 1 Slow Rollers and Fundamentals

◓BEGINNER

EQUIPMENT   12 cones; 1 bucket of baseballs; and an assistant coach, a parent, or a receiving net. Set up an appropriate number of cones, approximately 3 to 5 feet (90 to 150 cm) apart, to be used during discussion and teaching. Also, set up a triangle of cones for the ground-ball execution (slow rollers) part of the drill. Athletes will line up behind the point of the triangle, and the athlete whose turn it is will step forward in between the other two cones.

PURPOSE   This drill teaches basic ground-ball fundamentals and can be used to introduce the concepts of the ready position, the approach, and the fielding triangle.

PROCEDURE   *Part 1: Teaching.* Each athlete steps behind a cone; the cones are set up laterally in the fielding area, several feet apart (see figure *a*). The goal here is for each athlete to see and understand the breakdown of the series of movements required to field a ground ball. Provide a general overview of these movements. Before using any live ground balls, you should introduce and teach the steps for properly fielding a ground ball:

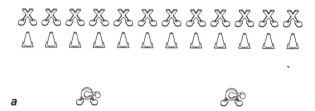

a

1. Ready position. All athletes step behind their cone. As a group, work through the right, left, hop rhythm of getting into the ready position. Allow the athletes to take turns yelling, stomping, or growling in their own special way.

2. Approach. Again as a group, move from the ready position along the proper path for approaching a ground ball.

3. Fielding triangle. Have the athletes physically draw their own triangle! After explaining the correct positioning, have the athletes get dirty and draw lines from their feet to their hands and in between their feet as well. The athletes should step back, compare triangles, and then jump into the fielding triangle and repeat.

4. Pop, shuffle, throw. Get ready for part 2 of this drill (slow rollers) by combining all the pieces. Have the athletes practice assuming the ready position, taking an approach, and moving into the fielding position. Next, begin instruction on the three movements taken *after* fielding the baseball.

Part 2: Slow rollers. Move from the teaching cones to a set of cones in the shape of a triangle near the fielding area (or reposition the teaching cones). On cue, athletes move forward and present their ready position in order to receive a ground ball (do not roll a ground ball until the athlete has achieved the ready position) (see figure *b*). Keep the pace slow and controlled, carefully monitoring proper execution while making sure that the athletes are enjoying themselves. Increase the pace and involve throws to a coach or net as appropriate.

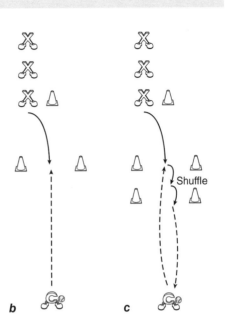

VARIATIONS

1. *Freeze movements.* If the coaching focus is on *instruction,* include freezes in the athlete's movements (broken movements). After the athlete moves into the *ready position,* roll the ground ball and have the athlete freeze after fielding the ball. Here, the athlete should be in the proper *fielding triangle.* After instructing the athlete on any necessary adjustments, you should then have him perform the *step* correctly. Then, verbally direct a *shuffle* and a *throw.*

2. *Momentum shuffles.* To show the importance of gaining momentum, building power, and directing the throw, you should now require the athletes to perform mandatory shuffles on each ground ball. Place two cones well in front of the fielding area, and instruct athletes to shuffle past the cones before making a throw (see figure *c*). This can be four or five shuffles in length. Have the athletes really gain speed and observe the throws. You should see the flight of the ball get straighter and straighter as the athletes get more power behind the throw. Over time, decrease the number of mandatory shuffles from three, down to two, and finally to one. Be sure to point out that the runner will dictate if an infielder needs to move quickly and get rid of the ball.

(continued)

3. *Forehands and backhands.* Include various types of ground balls, and force the athletes to field the baseball on either side of the body. A ground ball fielded off to the glove side of the body is called a forehand (photo *a*). A ball on the throwing-hand side of the body, requiring the fielder to take a crossover step, is commonly referred to as a backhand (similar to tennis) (photo *b*).

COACHING POINTS *Keywords.* Keywords are single words or phrases that can assist young athletes in remembering and retaining instruction. Emphasize keywords during every drill in order to help athletes remember proper technique later in the season. For example, use the term *alligator hands* to trigger proper position of the hands at the *fielding triangle* (another keyword). These phrases or words should be consistent between you and your assistant coaches, and they are often fairly consistent across the entire baseball world.

Drill 2 Dueling Fungoes

⚾⚾ INTERMEDIATE

EQUIPMENT   Two bats (fungoes), two buckets of baseballs (as many balls as possible), a catch net, and an assistant coach or parent

PURPOSE   This drill maximizes the number of ground balls for each athlete in a short amount of time. Competition keeps this drill extremely enjoyable, and instruction can be involved as much as you like.

PROCEDURE   The Dueling Fungoes drill is applicable to athletes of all ages and involves the entire team. Separate athletes into two groups and encourage friendly competition. Athletes should also be encouraged to maintain proper fielding fundamentals. Dueling Fungoes can be done with two coaches competing along with their respective teams or with a single coach hitting or rolling ground balls to both lines of athletes.

The rules are very simple: Split the group into two even teams. One team lines up behind a cone placed in between the pitcher's mound and first base. The other team lines up behind a cone placed in between the pitcher's mound and third base. A target net is placed just behind home plate; this net will serve as the "basket." Coaches line up on either side of the catch net (or a single coach can pick a side) in position to hit ground balls to the athletes (see figure a).

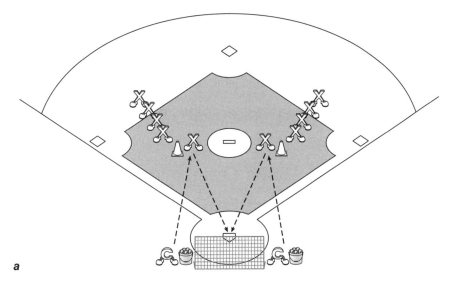

a

If an athlete makes a throw into the catch net, he earns a point for his team! With both teams lined up behind their respective cones, the first athlete steps forward and into the ready position. Coaches take turns hitting ground balls and checking fundamentals. Athletes are simply to field the ground ball correctly, shuffle their feet, make an aggressive throw,

(continued)

and then return to the end of the line. If the ball ends up in the net, that athlete's team earns a point. The first team to reach a determined number is the victor. The coaches need to be loud and create energy—this drill is fast paced. Athletes love the chance to compete against one another and avoid doing push-ups or picking up baseballs!

VARIATIONS

1. To challenge athletes, add a rule that the fielder must execute proper technique (alligator hands, fielding triangle, shuffle step) or the throw will not count. For example, if an athlete fields a ground ball with one hand and lets loose a throw, you should scream, "No point!" When the team complains and argues after the ball hits the target, you can coolly and calmly explain, "No fundamentals . . . no points." You can sure bet that the next time this athlete steps up to field a ground ball, he will be using two hands. Why? Because he wants to make you happy? Heck no, he wants a point!

2. The advanced version of Dueling Fungoes involves an entire team in infield practice using multiple ground balls and the infield diamond. The head-to-head competition is removed, but the execution challenge is significantly increased. Two coaches hit ground balls, each working with two positions around the infield (see figure *b*). One coach hits from the third-base side of home plate, and the other hits from the first-base side of the plate. Place athletes at the infield positions (third base, shortstop, second base, and first base); also place a receiver at both first and second base. The receivers should be adults if at all possible.

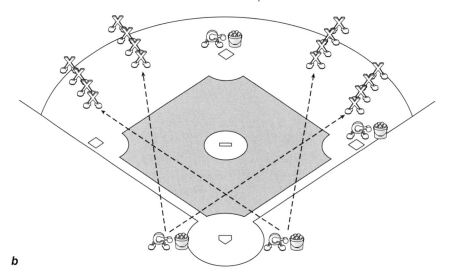

b

- **Segment 1.** The coach on the third-base side will hit ground balls to the shortstop and first-base player, who will then feed to the receiver standing at the second-base bag (simulating the throw when starting a double play). The coach on the first-base side will hit ground balls to the third-base and second-base players, who will throw across to the receiver at first base.
- **Segment 2.** Coaches hit to the same positions, but the feeds are reversed. The shortstop and first-base player now throw to the receiver at first base. The third-base and second-base players now feed to the second-base bag.

Coaches alternate hitting ground balls, ensuring that a quick pace is maintained. Receivers should stay with their respective coach, expecting throws from alternating positions. When the feeds switch, receivers will take throws from new positions. Watch out for athletes charging ground balls and getting in the way of throws to different bases.

COACHING POINTS *Safety first.* With throws going everywhere, this drill can quickly become chaos. Be sure that the receiving coach pays attention and stays with you at all times. If possible, place an empty bucket at the second-base bag for the receiving coach to drop baseballs into. Do the same thing just behind first base. As soon as you run out of baseballs, switch your empty bucket for the full bucket at second or first base.

Drill 3 Box Drills

⊕BEGINNER

EQUIPMENT   Four cones, one baseball (for each four-corner area)

PURPOSE   This drill allows for a variety of movements in a confined space. Drill ground-ball technique, footwork, quick hands (transfer), and performance under pressure. As with most of these drills, competition and timing can increase drill intensity and enjoyment.

PROCEDURE   Set up a small square with cones 30 to 40 feet (9 to 12 m) apart, and distribute your athletes evenly at each cone. You may set up two boxes if necessary to involve the entire team. Begin by rolling the ground ball to a specific athlete. His task is to move and receive the baseball in the fielding triangle position, shuffle his feet, and roll a ground ball to the athlete on his left (see the figure). Continue this process until you are pleased with the athletes' execution. To add a workout component, have each athlete "follow his toss." After the athlete rolls the ball to his left, he follows that baseball and sprints to the next cone.

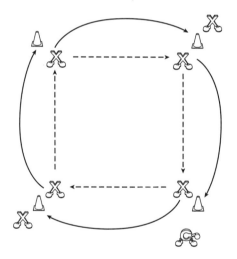

VARIATIONS

1. Include a variety of throws, ground balls, tags, and so on. You can also reverse the direction. Instruct athletes to turn right and circulate the baseball in a counterclockwise fashion (when viewing from above). This requires the feet to literally jump and replace each other—a movement called the *reverse pivot.*

2. Use the full diamond to increase the distance of throws, and add competition by setting goals for the number of throws without an error or the number of throws in a certain time period. Place infielders at bases, and catchers can even get in a crouch and come out to throw. Set goals for the number of throws *and* catches without an error. Add a reward or penalty to increase pressure and mimic game stresses; for example, if the athletes achieve 10 throws without an error, they can avoid running after practice. Be sure to set a realistic time limit.

COACHING POINTS *Space management.* The Box drill is a great drill when you have limited space. Requiring only a small patch of grass, this drill can be done as one of several stations during station instruction, and it can take place in the outfield or even off of the main field area. If necessary, your team can stretch, run, and throw and then take part in several drills such as the Box drill before your field time begins. If your team is only allocated 60 or 90 minutes of field time, begin your practice in a nearby open area and use drills that enable you to make good use of the space available.

Drill 4 Ground Ball–Quick Catch

BEGINNER

EQUIPMENT   One cone, one baseball (for each line)

PURPOSE   This drill can be used to work on fielding footwork, quick hands, and other movements required to move from the receiving position to a throwing position quickly and efficiently. It can be executed in any small grassy or infield area and takes little setup time.

PROCEDURE   Especially with young athletes, this drill is a great way to develop baseball athleticism. Break the athletes into as many groups as possible and line them up behind a single cone. For example, if you have three coaches, you may divide the team into three lines of four athletes each. If you have two coaches, you would have two lines of six athletes. Each athlete will receive a rolled ground ball, followed by a throw, followed by a second ground ball, a second throw, and so on. With each ball fielded or caught, the athlete should field and separate while his feet quickly jump pivot into a throwing position toward the target. After making a throw, the athlete should jump back to a ready position to accept the next ball.

Alternating between ground balls and regular throws, the athlete should receive three to five of each (ground ball, quick catch, ground ball, quick catch, and so on). Emphasize a quick pop, where the feet quickly shuffle from fielding triangle to throwing position. The same holds true for a quick catch—the hands catch first then separate immediately while the feet jump pivot into position.

VARIATIONS   *Added competition.* To increase pressure and enhance competition, measure the amount of time it takes for each athlete to complete a given number of repetitions. Assuming there are two coaches, this means two lines of six athletes each. To reduce the amount of time that athletes spend waiting in lines, cut the number of ground ball and quick catch repetitions down to three each. Start the clock when you roll the first ground ball, and stop it after you receive the final return throw. Compare this time for all the athletes, and include some sort of reward or prize for the shortest time.

COACHING POINTS   This is a good drill to incorporate into station instruction, and it is a perfect fit for the time immediately after team warm-up. This time was referred to earlier as Five Minutes for Fielding. The Ground Ball–Quick Catch drill is a good way to refresh ground-ball fundamentals quickly, especially if the practice plan calls for more advanced instruction later in the afternoon.

Drill 5 Double-Play Feeds

⚾⚾⚾ ADVANCED

EQUIPMENT   One bucket of baseballs, two cones, one catch net or assistant coach

PURPOSE   This drill can be used to work on ground-ball mechanics as well as double-play feeds to second base. Forehand and backhand fielding technique can also be easily involved.

PROCEDURE   This drill is run for both the shortstop and second-base position.

SHORTSTOP POSITION   Place a catch net or an assistant coach just in front of the second-base bag. Athletes line up behind a single cone that is placed near the shortstop position on the cut of the infield grass. The first athlete steps in front of the cone and gets into the ready position (right, left, hop). Begin by drilling the footwork and movements of the shortstop position's double-play feeds. Do this by first rolling ground balls directly at the athletes (see the figure).

Before beginning the repetitions, you should briefly discuss the two main shortstop feeds—the underhand flip and the overhand throw. The repetitions should begin with the athletes performing the underhand flip first. The overhand toss (or "dart") will come next, as will more difficult ground balls and finally the feeds made from the second-base position. Once the fundamentals have been discussed and the keywords emphasized, drill underhand flips for four or five minutes and then switch to the overhand toss.

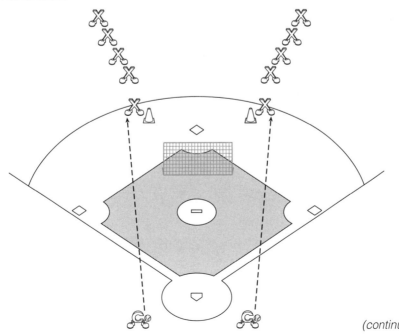

(continued)

- **Underhand flip.** Technically speaking, an underhand flip will be used when the ball is hit directly at the shortstop (or hit to his left, closer to the bag). This requires a soft toss that can be easily handled by the second baseman. Hence, an underhand flip is used. After fielding the ball, the athlete crosses the right foot over the left foot in the direction of second base. The athlete performs the underhand toss using a stiff wrist and high follow-through and should carry the hand toward second base for several steps after making the toss in order to ensure a soft and easily handled feed (see the photo). For the drill, athletes are in one line. Roll the ball directly to the athletes (or just to their left side). The athlete should field the baseball, separate, and flip (right foot moves toward the target, right hand flips) to throw to the net or athlete at the second-base bag.

- **Overhand toss.** An overhand throw is only used if the distance to be covered is large enough. Fundamentally, that means that an overhand throw is used when the ball is hit to the right of the shortstop's position. This is a short, controlled toss, often referred to as a dart. For young athletes, you should be sure to explain these simple rules:
  1. If the ball is toward the bag (to the athlete's left), an underhand flip is used.
  2. If the ball is away from the bag (to the athlete's right), an overhand toss is used.

3. If the ball is directly at the athlete, either throw may be used (the athlete should surround and flip if possible).

Athletes line up single file once again behind the position cone. Roll a ground ball just to the athlete's right side. The athlete should field the baseball, separate and open up, and deliver a strike to the net or athlete at the second-base bag. Athletes should keep the feet planted at first, and they should open up the left foot as appropriate.

SECOND-BASE POSITION   Focus on the footwork, movements, and throws made from the second-base position. Briefly discuss the two main second-base feeds (underhand flip and overhand toss with a reverse pivot) before beginning the repetitions for the underhand flip.

- **Underhand flip.** The underhand flip is used when the ball is hit to the second-base player's right. The athlete uses a left-foot crossover (left foot, right hand). For the drill, athletes are in one line. Roll the ball to the athlete's right side. The athlete should field the baseball, separate, and execute a left-foot crossover step to deliver a soft feed to the net or athlete representing the shortstop at the second-base bag.

- **Overhand toss.** The overhand toss is used when the ball is hit to the second-base player's left (requiring a reverse pivot). The feet must turn all the way around to a throwing position toward second base (the hands separate, then the feet pivot). For the drill, athletes are in one line. Roll the ball to the athlete's left side. The athlete should field the baseball, get the feet all the way around, and deliver a strike to the net or athlete representing the shortstop at the second-base bag.

VARIATIONS

1. *Be an athlete—Either/Or Feeds.* Discuss that infielders must be athletes and must think on their feet. A ground ball hit right at the athlete requires the athlete to make a decision on which feed to use (overhand versus underhand). If the ball is hit softly, a fielder can take a surrounding approach and create an underhand feed. If the ball is hit sharply, this may not be possible. Alternate between left and right feeds and then roll some directly at the athletes to force an athletic decision. Encourage the kids to play the game and get a feel for which feed is appropriate.

(continued)

2. *Live ground balls to receiver.* Use batted balls and then also include a live feed to a second-base receiver. Later in the season, you can even have the athletes turn a full double play. It can be very fulfilling to take young infielders through the developmental steps of fielding ground balls. Even at the youngest age levels, athletes can learn to execute a complete double play. Just be careful of who is throwing to whom and which athletes you need to be careful with. When using live feeds, have the athletes rotate between positions regularly to ensure that they all experience the different responsibilities at each area.

COACHING POINTS *Side-by-side cones.* A great way to start each station is for athletes to line up between the side-by-side cones. At each station, place two cones just off to the side of the area where the kids are going to be doing the drill. When the group jogs up to your station, instruct them to line up, side by side, between the two cones. They can hold their arms out to ensure that there's enough space in between each athlete. Then they wait to receive instruction. Because you want to discuss both the specifics of the drill to be done and the fundamental techniques to be learned, placing the athletes in a horizontal line facing you allows for quick discussion without distraction. Take time at the first practice or two to explain the concept of side-by-side cones. This will quickly become second nature for the athletes, and you will avoid any time lost to herding or corralling.

The Coach's Clipboard

✔ Understand first, coach second. Study and understand the fundamentals of fielding a ground ball before applying that information to the coaching process.

✔ Teach and then drill. Describe and coach the movements of fielding a ground ball before moving into drills (instruction versus repetition).

✔ Teach the fundamentals of fielding a ground ball: ready position; approach; fielding triangle; and step, shuffle, and throw.

✔ Encourage a team ready position to get 20 eyeballs looking at the ball in play.

✔ Teach a fielding triangle to give athletes the best chance of catching a ground ball cleanly.

✔ Let it rip! Athletes need to aggressively shuffle toward their target and unleash a full throw.

✔ Start slowly and encourage proper fundamentals before involving batted balls or an increased pace.

✔ Use keywords to help athletes remember instruction.

✔ Use side-by-side cones to start each fielding station quickly without distractions.

✔ Practice defense before offense—kids can always find the energy to hit.

Developing Outfield Skills With 5 Simple Drills

This chapter can be boiled down to three simple words, which, when combined, can become an extremely challenging task: *catch . . . the . . . ball.* We could have called this chapter "Catching" just as easily, but we didn't want to mislead readers into thinking we'll be discussing wearing a mask and a chest protector. This chapter covers the art of teaching kids to catch the baseball!

In the case of beginning baseball players, any ball that reaches a height three inches above the hat will hereby be referred to as a fly ball. The main challenge facing you as a coach is to create an atmosphere of comfort and growth where the athletes can feel assured that they won't be hurt. Athletes need help to put aside their fear of being hit by the baseball so that all of their energy can be positively placed on learning to catch it (and having fun while doing so). You, as a coach, get to focus on finding that glove! Underhand or overhand, short tosses or high fly balls, one of the most valuable skills a coach can have is throwing the ball so that it finds the web of the glove.

Fly Ball 101

To better understand the fly ball, let's first discuss the fundamentals that our little all-stars must learn in order to become what we envision them turning into—the baseball outfielder:

1. Ready position
2. Drop step and read
3. Crossover
4. Go!

Ready Position

Similar to the infielders, all outfielders should be encouraged to focus their eyes on the home plate area just as the pitch is released (figure 4.1a). The outfielders can also use the same "right, left, hop" footwork to ensure that they are on the balls of their feet and ready to react. Remember that the outfield provides the most stiff competition for the athletes' attention on the ready position—the outfielders can be easily distracted by butterflies and gopher holes. In tee ball, each team is encouraged to place an assistant coach in the outfield to assist with positioning and paying attention. Well-trained outfielders, even at the tee ball level, can shake the earth together with the best of the infielders.

Drop Step and Read

First step back! Any time a ball is hit in the air off the bat, an athlete's first step should be back (figure 4.1b). Specifically, on a ball to his right side, the athlete should step back with his right leg and open up to judge distance. On a ball hit in the air to his left, the athlete should drop-step with his left leg. The next task is to read how hard the ball is hit in order to decide whether to continue back on the baseball or reverse direction and charge in. Any fly ball hit short will require the athlete to move in.

Crossover

For a ball hit behind the outfielder, the athlete should take a drop step followed by a crossover step (figure 4.1c). On a ball to the outfielder's right, the drop step will be with the right foot, and the subsequent crossover step will be with the left foot. For a ball hit to the outfielder's left, the drop step will be with the left foot, and the subsequent crossover step will be with the right foot. This may sound complicated, but it's simple and it works! If and when the athletes are ready, you *can* teach these first two steps slowly and correctly.

Go!

Finally, the outfielder must run down the baseball and make the catch (figure 4.1*d*). After taking the drop step and reading the ball—and crossing over if going back—the athlete must then go get it!

Figure 4.1 *(a)* Ready position, *(b)* drop step, *(c)* crossover, and *(d)* go!

Teaching Beginning Receiving—Catching 101

Now that you know the fundamentals of an outfielder, you also need to understand that teaching fly-ball technique is something that can only be done when athletes are comfortable catching the ball. Although we'd like our athletes to run, catch, and throw like Willie Mays (and to reach the point where our practice plans cover drop steps and crossovers), coaches first need to address receiving—also known as the art of catching the ball.

Catching the ball is simple in theory and difficult in reality. Young athletes have an inherent fear of being hit by the baseball, and they usually have a tough time judging speed and distance. Judging trajectory and anticipating where a fly ball will land can take years and years of practice. When trying to teach a team how to receive a fly ball, you need to understand the challenges that young athletes face.

Using tennis balls, safety baseballs, or even a rolled-up sock, begin by simply tossing looping throws away from the athlete's body. An athlete's focus needs to be dedicated to catching the ball and should not be on getting hit. This means that tosses should be made away from the head of the athletes. In addition, you should initially put very little pressure on the athletes to perform proper fundamentals or mechanics. Allow youngsters to use two hands, even if they are not using gloves, because the goal is to build confidence. Athletic abilities will vary greatly among the players, so you may want to subtly break the team into groups based on talent level. Or, you can vary the difficulty of your tosses to match the talent level of the individual athlete.

Initially, you need to allow athletes to catch the ball in whatever way they are comfortable. Being careful not to throw the ball too high, you first need to build the athletes' confidence in receiving before you push for technique. Athletes need lots and lots of practice catching fly balls—there is no magic pill or secret drill to skip this process.

Two Hands Versus One Hand

Encourage athletes to use two hands when catching a baseball. The glove hand catches the ball while the throwing hand keeps the ball in the glove. There are times when it's more appropriate to go to the ball with only the glove arm—for example, when making catches on the run or when extending for a ball away from the body. However, you should teach athletes to catch with two hands on all beginning receiving drills.

Avoiding the Backpedal

Athletes should not backpedal on any fly ball over their heads. Plain and simple, backpedaling leads to reverse somersaults and should be avoided at all costs. Establish a "no backpedal" rule where violators are required to take a lap around the field while running backward.

Communication

Initially, your role as a coach is to introduce the need for "calling" a fly ball. To avoid collisions, athletes should use the common "I got it, I got it, I got it" (three times) to let everyone know they will be attempting to catch the ball. A simple rule for outfield play is that the ball must be called by an athlete before it starts the downward flight. Encourage aggressive behavior because you want your players not to be afraid to make mistakes. However, athletes need to learn to respect their teammates and to back off if someone else calls the baseball.

Who Should Catch What?

Center fielders have priority over corner outfielders on balls hit into the outfield. All outfielders have priority over infielders on those balls hit in between the infield and outfield. These rules hold true for all levels of baseball, but for youth baseball, the best athletes may end up playing middle infield and will make more catches in the shallow outfield area. Teach the game the right way . . . and then take the outs wherever you can get them.

Drill 1 Thumbs Up, Pinkies Down

⊘BEGINNER

EQUIPMENT   One bucket of baseballs, tennis balls, or safety baseballs; cones

PURPOSE   This drill teaches the receiving position of the hands. It also provides an opportunity to teach athletes to use two hands when catching a ball.

PROCEDURE   Teach the athletes how to position their hands to most easily catch a baseball. Any ball above the belt requires that the thumbs be brought closer together so that the fingers point up to the sky (photo *a*). This ensures that two hands are used to catch the ball. Any ball below the belt requires that the pinkies be brought together (fingers point down to the ground) (photo *b*).

With the athletes facing you between the side-by-side cones, move through the receiving positions as a group. When you point up, the athletes should move their hands up, connecting their thumbs. When you point down, the athletes should flip their hands around so that the pinkies touch. The first part of this drill is simply to feel the hands turn over and move from "thumbs" to "pinkies." The second part of the drill is to understand the concept of when to use each position—on a ball above the belt, use thumbs; on a ball below the belt, use pinkies.

VARIATIONS

1. *Live tosses.* Toss the ball in predictable locations so athletes can practice moving to the baseball. Have them start with their hands out at their sides, pointing straight out in front of their bodies with the palms facing each other. This way they can feel the hands move up and down from the same starting location.

2. *Carry the tray.* Instruct athletes to assume a position similar to a waiter carrying a tray full of burgers and fries. The palm of the glove hand should face the sky. Once the athletes are in that position, you should toss the baseball on an arc so that it will land just behind the athlete's glove-side shoulder. Stand 10 to 15 feet (3.0 to 4.5 m) in front of the athlete. Be sure to keep the tosses away from the athlete's head. Encourage athletes to make sure the throwing hand clamps down on the baseball once it enters into the glove webbing.

COACHING POINTS   *Eyes up.* Many young athletes will close their eyes or take their eyes off of a flying baseball. Obviously, this is a huge hindrance to their receiving ability and is a habit that must be broken. Use lots of patience and be sure to toss the ball well away from the body. As the athlete slowly learns to trust you and grows confident that the ball will not be thrown at him, his focus can naturally turn to catching the ball. Those athletes who are unsure about their own ability to catch the ball cannot waste any energy worrying about whether the ball will be tossed at them.

Drill 2 Four-Corners Receiving

EQUIPMENT   Two cones; one bucket of baseballs, tennis balls, or safety baseballs

PURPOSE   This drill teaches basic receiving movements of the hands.

PROCEDURE   Four-Corners Receiving can be done with rolled-up socks, tennis balls, safety balls, or regular baseballs (you'll know which ball to use). Break the squad into as many lines as you have assistant coaches. Then, each coach tosses balls to the athlete standing in front of him or her. Athletes set their feet and receive throws. With slow and controlled movements, the coaches should toss the ball accurately to the four receiving areas:

1. Beyond the right shoulder (photo *a*)
2. Beyond the left shoulder (photo *b*)
3. To the right thigh (photo *c*)
4. To the left thigh (photo *d*)

The athlete should use the thumbs-up or pinkies-down rule to receive at the four locations. Move the throws from area to area in a predictable manner. Over time, the locations can be thrown at random and with higher velocity to increase difficulty. Start by forcing the athletes to use two hands and then challenge them to perform one-handed receiving. Athletes should focus all their energy on simply catching the baseball. Use loads of positive language and encourage kids *not* to be afraid. The only way to improve is to experience dropping the baseball (and catching it!).

VARIATIONS

1. *Hand behind the back.* Instruct the athlete to place his throwing hand behind his back and to move to the baseball with only the glove hand. Encourage an athletic rhythm and really work to perfect the amount of arc you place on each toss to the athlete. This is the aforementioned coaching art of finding the glove.

(continued)

2. *Varied locations.* Slowly increase the pace of the tossed fly balls and alter the location of those tosses. Be sure to start in a predictable order (to help the athletes build confidence and positive vibes), and then pour on the challenge with tosses to varied locations.

3. *No glove.* Have the athletes take the glove off to work on receiving with a soft touch (see photo *e*). Athletes may use one or two hands. This variation can be a good way to challenge those athletes who are naturally more athletic than other teammates.

COACHING POINTS *Stick and move.* Remember to stay positive and not dwell on a specific athlete or a specific spot where an athlete is struggling to make catches. If you toss 17 baseballs in a row to the spot where Little Johnny is having a difficult time catching, Little Johnny won't be the only one frustrated. This will test the patience of those other kids waiting in line, anyone watching the drill, and even yourself. After 3 or 4 unsuccessful tosses to a location, simply move on and look to draw attention away from that struggle and onto something positive. Use as many baseballs as possible so you can keep the drill moving quickly and keep the kids rotating in and out of the action.

Drill 3 Quarterback Tosses

⚾⚾ INTERMEDIATE

EQUIPMENT   Baseballs and cones

PURPOSE   This drill can be used to add footwork fundamentals to receiving practice.

PROCEDURE   Hold a baseball in your throwing hand. The athlete should stand directly in front of you (facing you) and should follow your cues. Begin by pointing over either the athlete's right or left shoulder. Depending on where you point, the athlete should take a *drop step* with that foot, opening up in anticipation of a fly ball in that direction (as if reading the ball off of the bat). Next, instruct the athlete to take a *crossover step* and freeze. Then, and only then, toss a ball in the same direction so the athlete can move back on the ball and make the catch.

VARIATIONS

1. *One movement.* Eliminate the freeze at the drop step or crossover movements. Point in a direction and allow the athlete to move on his own. Toss the ball an appropriate height and then focus your coaching on the athlete's ability to catch the baseball.

2. *In-and-out.* Incorporate fly balls where the athlete must move in to catch the ball. Be sure that the athlete's first step is still back—and with the correct foot (based on where you point). But then mix in balls where the athletes must move in as well as fly balls over their shoulder.

3. *Football patterns.* Dig deep to muster up your inner Tom Brady or Joe Montana. Athletes line up behind a cone that is 20 to 30 feet (6 to 9 m) away from the coach; each athlete has a baseball. The first athlete runs toward the coach, underhand tosses the ball to the coach, and then continues running to receive a football pass. After catching (or attempting to catch) the baseball, athletes can form a line on the other side of the area or return to the beginning line. See the figure.

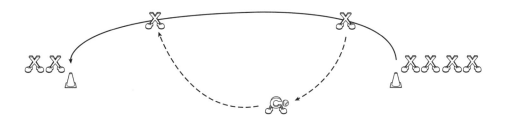

(continued)

COACHING POINTS

1. *Keeping the head steady.* Outfielders are taught to run on the balls of their feet to keep their eyes from bouncing. Discuss the importance of keeping the head steady. Have athletes attempt to run with soft feet so that the eyes remain level. If the athlete's eyes bounce while running, the fly ball will also appear to bounce.

2. *Encourage effort.* Take fear of failure out of the drill by celebrating effort. Even if the ball is dropped (physical error), stay positive and keep the kids aggressive in their efforts to catch it. That being said, if an athlete doesn't go hard for a pass (mental error), you may unleash the high school football coach inside of you—tight shorts, whistle, clipboard, and all!

Drill 4 Kick Back Jack

EQUIPMENT   Wiffle balls or rolled-up socks (each rolled up into a ball), baseball gloves

PURPOSE   This drill teaches athletes to use proper form when catching a ball.

PROCEDURE   The athlete lies down on the grass, flat on his back. From the horizontal position, proper receiving form can be achieved by reaching straight up and opening the glove to the sky (the waiter-with-tray position). Using a Wiffle ball or a rolled-up sock, stand next to the athlete and softly drop or toss the sock toward the glove side of the athlete. Be sure that the fear factor is avoided by dropping the sock away from the head. Also make sure that the athlete uses two hands to move to the falling sock.

VARIATIONS

1. *Varied location.* Move the tosses from side to side so the athlete has to move the glove around the four corners of receiving. Have the athlete take the glove off and do this drill barehanded.
2. *Self-toss.* After several practices, athletes should be able to toss the socks on their own. Add competition to see how many tosses the athletes can do without letting the sock touch the ground.

COACHING POINTS   The Kick Back Jack drill is a great example of how parents can be incorporated into your practice plan. Any available body can assist with dropping a sock! Use them—they'd rather help than stand around.

Drill 5 Tennis Racket Fly Balls

EQUIPMENT   Tennis racket, tennis balls, cones

PURPOSE   Use the racket and tennis balls to raise the height of the fly ball and increase the associated challenges. You can easily control direction and distance, and you can challenge athletes to communicate in calling for the ball. By sending athletes in a particular direction, you can use this drill to work on catching on the run.

PROCEDURE   Use the tennis racket to hit fly balls accurately and effectively. This saves the time that is often wasted on poorly hit fly balls when using a bat.

VARIATIONS

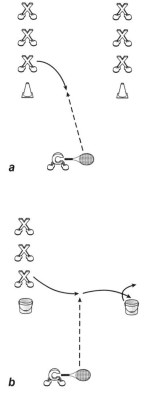

1. *Communication.* Divide the athletes into two lines and start each line behind a cone. Hit the ball in between the cones and allow the athletes to call for and then catch the fly balls (see figure *a*). Begin by alternating priority between the two lines, then move on to the challenge of requiring the athletes to appropriately call for the ball based on who is closer to it.

2. *Bucket to bucket.* Place two buckets 50 to 75 feet (15 to 22 m) apart from each other. The athletes are lined up behind one bucket. The first athlete steps out in front and gets into a ready position (right, left, hop). Hit a fly ball in between the buckets so that the athlete must run underneath the ball. After properly catching the fly ball, the athlete should carry and drop the ball into the other bucket (see figure *b*). For increased energy, add difficulty or a points competition with throws to a target.

COACHING POINTS   *Put down the bat.* Your ego does not need the beating! It's difficult enough to hit a fly ball—let alone hit the fly ball with the proper height and accuracy. These drills are most effective and safe when you use hand-tossed fly balls. And when you need a little help, break out the tennis racket. The kids will think it's fun and unique to see a tennis racket on the baseball field. Remember, novelty is key when keeping kids entertained and enjoying themselves.

The Coach's Clipboard

✔ Remove the fear of being hit by tossing fly balls away from the athlete's head.

✔ Allow athletes to catch the ball naturally before you add fundamentals or teach technique.

✔ Teach the fundamentals of catching a fly ball: ready position, drop step and read, crossover, and go.

✔ Teach the proper hand positions for catching a fly ball: thumbs up for a ball above the belt; pinkies down for a ball below the belt.

✔ Put safety first. Use rolled-up socks, tennis balls, or safety balls before attempting the drills with base-balls.

✔ Encourage athletes to communicate by calling all fly balls. They should take charge and be loud.

✔ Know your talent levels, and challenge the athletes accordingly.

✔ Teach your waiters to carry trays when catching the ball.

✔ Involve outfield positions and instruction when training on fly balls (who catches what?).

✔ Assign funwork—enjoyable homework.

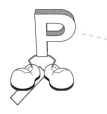

Developing Throwing Skills With 5 Simple Drills

Teaching young baseball players to throw correctly takes patience, lots of smiling, and a good sense of humor. Athletes come in all shapes and sizes, and their respective throwing styles can vary just as much. Fortunately, there *are* a handful of rules that all athletes should follow when throwing. These rules still allow each kid to be himself. Let's examine these throwing guidelines and then walk through some drills to assist with teaching young ballplayers to throw correctly.

Throwing 101

Basic throwing can be broken down into the positioning of the body and then the action of the arm itself. With the youngest baseball players, most of your attention will be focused on getting an athlete into the best throwing *position* possible. Accept the challenge of teaching athletes to move their feet correctly and to reach their arms in the proper direction—then hope for the best once the arm reaches back to throw!

Proper Grip

For the smallest hands, the positioning on the baseball may not make much of a difference. However, when you are working to provide athletes with every chance to succeed, teaching the proper grip simply can't hurt—it can only help.

Teach athletes to use the four-seam grip (figure 5.1). This grip, when the throw is executed correctly, leaves the hand with the straightest path and the most speed possible. We're trying to help these kids throw the ball straight—every bit helps. The ball is gripped across two of the wide seams (the "horseshoe" or "smile"), and the fingers on top of the ball (two or three) rest on top of the stitches, approximately a half inch (1.5 cm) apart. You can use this key phrase: "Give the smile braces!" The thumb is tucked underneath the ball, resting on

Figure 5.1   Four-seam grip.

or near a bottom seam. As the size of a pitcher's hand increases, there should be enough space between the palm and the baseball to move a finger in and out of the space between the thumb and the index finger.

Two Fingers on Top

Young athletes tend to use three (or even four) fingers when gripping the baseball. It makes sense that an athlete with small hands will use the grip that feels most comfortable—one that will not stretch the fingers out. Typically, this grip ends up with three fingers on top of the ball (index, middle, and ring fingers) and two fingers underneath it. But let's be honest, most of the time, a young athlete is not putting much thought into how the ball is gripped at all. Whenever possible, you should arm that athlete with a plan.

Try this: Ask your athletes how many big leaguers throw a fastball with three fingers. When they respond with silence, confirm that the answer is zero. Then communicate that the faster they can get comfortable using two fingers on top of the baseball, the closer they are to the big leagues. If the little guy's hands really are that small, then fine, he can use three fingers on top. Just be sure to let him know that the goal is to switch to a two-finger grip as soon as possible. The next Joe Torre is not going to wait around forever for him to reach the big leagues.

Power Position

Every good throw begins with proper positioning of the feet. Whether a player has just slickly fielded a ground ball or bravely stood underneath a fly ball, the player will move into the power position before releasing a throw. *Teaching* beginning throwing starts here—at the power position.

The power position (figure 5.2) prepares the rocket to launch—it is a loaded, powerful position screaming of strength, accuracy, and efficiency. This ball has been cleared for takeoff, and there is no flight plan whatsoever. Countdown is commencing: 3 . . . 2 . . . 1 . . . launch. Look out above, below, to the left, or possibly to the right!

Figure 5.2   Power position.

Luckily, the power position can help, and it can also be easily taught. Teaching the power position is the fastest way to corral a wild thrower, to improve throwing accuracy, and to build confidence in both throwers and receivers. The power position has four components, which come together to form a big X:

- **Glove arm up:** The glove arm should be high (above shoulder height) and pointed in the direction of the target.

- **Throwing arm held high with a slight bend:** The baseball should point directly away from the body with the fingers on top of the ball. Call this the cobra and encourage sound effects.

- **Front foot closed and up on the toes:** The side of the front shoe should point to the target (referred to as closed)—and the athlete should be up on the toes!

- **Back leg supporting most of the weight:** The majority of an athlete's weight should rest, loaded, on the back leg. This is the reason why the athlete should step lightly on the front foot and use only the toes or ball of the foot to rest. Doing this helps to ensure that the athlete has kept his weight over the back leg.

From the power position, an athlete is ready to unleash fury on the baseball. A coach's job is to encourage athletes to have an aggressive release without fear of making a mistake. At times, it's fun to celebrate wild throws, realizing that the youngsters need to develop confidence in throwing the ball hard and with pace. As long as you don't actively encourage wild throws, finding the time to chuckle and celebrate a crazy toss may be the only thing that keeps your own sanity. When teaching throwing, be sure to create a fun environment where athletes will not fear making an aggressive attempt. If they are genuinely giving you effort to make a good throw, you've done all that you can do.

A proper power position has the athlete holding a majority of his weight on the back leg. As the body steps and moves forward to throw, the arm follows a top-to-bottom path. Here is a common phrase that most coaches are familiar with, even if they've never put on a uniform: "Get on top . . . throw over the top . . . no sidearm!" Well, it's true! Athletes should be encouraged to throw over the top, although the degree to which the arm actually travels from top to bottom will vary greatly. This should impart backspin on the baseball as the fingers pass from top to bottom behind the baseball, similar to the stroke of a paintbrush.

Throwing Absolutes

While respecting that each player is unique and has his own most comfortable arm angle, a coach should also keep in mind the following throwing absolutes that will help players stay safe and healthy while learning:

1. As the arm passes the head during a throw, the height of the throwing elbow should be at or above the throwing shoulder (figure 5.3a, see page 68). This means no sidearm throws.

2. At the release point, the throwing hand should be located in line with or outside the elbow (figure 5.3b). Commonly referred to as an athlete's arm angle, this means that the hand should not pass through directly next to the ear or head (no short arming).

3. Athletes should try to lead with the hand (figure 5.3c), and they should avoid dropping the arm and leading with the elbow. Think of this order as the athlete is throwing toward you: (1) hand, (2) arm, (3) body.

4. Throwing over the top, or top to bottom, helps alleviate stress on the elbow and helps athletes to keep their fingers on top of the baseball (figure 5.3d). There may come a time when you need to strike a little fear or respect into the athletes by sharing a couple stories of injuries. Keep any gory details out of it, and exaggerate as you see fit, but if necessary, you may have to "scare the athletes straight."

Finish and Follow-Through

Contrary to what many young baseball players will display, a fundamentally sound follow-through is not a 360-degree spin followed by a backward somersault. Instead, a good finish is a balanced and athletic position, with the arm following through completely and the body following suit. This ensures that an athlete has gained momentum and directed energy toward the desired target. *Throwing focus* could be an appropriate term for this directional movement. Heck, the word *focus* could probably be injected into every movement, topic, or drill in this book.

Following through is defined as the throwing arm continuing its path after releasing the baseball. The arm should end up near the outside of the opposite knee—as if a right-handed player was scratching an itch on the outside of the left knee (figure 5.4). Physically, this helps to keep the arm healthy by placing the workload of slowing the arm down after a throw onto the big muscles of the shoulder and back. Contrarily, cutting off the throwing motion without following through puts that workload onto the small muscles in the rear of the shoulder (this needs to be avoided

Figure 5.3 The "absolutely" perfect throw: *(a)* throwing elbow at or above throwing shoulder, *(b)* at release point, throwing hand in line with or outside elbow, *(c)* lead with throwing hand, and *(d)* throw over the top.

because it causes many athletes to experience fatigue, pain, or injury). Not only does following through help to keep the arm healthy, but a proper finish also leaves the body in a good fielding position for a return throw or play.

When athletes are learning to play catch, you can teach them the follow-through by having the athletes hold their finish position. The back of the throwing shoulder should face the target, and the feet should be roughly straight across. The focus of a good finish should be on following through with the arm and keeping balance with the legs. Simply put, young athletes need to be able to throw aggressively without falling over!

Figure 5.4 Follow-through.

Drill 1 Broken Throwing

EQUIPMENT   Baseball, partner

PURPOSE   This drill can be used to teach the basic body mechanics of throwing, with an emphasis on the power position.

PROCEDURE   Athletes are in throwing pairs. Half the athletes form one line along the foul line, and their partners are positioned 30 to 40 feet (9 to 12 m) away. Athletes along the line will start the drill with a baseball (thrower), and athletes on the other side will catch the throw (receiver).

Starting in the set position, the athletes wait for the coach's verbal signal to move to the power position. In the set position, the athlete's feet are shoulder-width apart, and the glove shoulder is pointing directly at the throwing partner. The hands are together in front of the chest, and the eyes are focused on the partner's waiting glove. This is very similar to a pitcher who has come set with a runner on first base (pitching from the stretch).

When the coach calls out "power," the athletes should take their stride, break their hands, and then freeze. This is the power position. At this point, check the four body parts and their positioning:

- **Glove arm:** high and in the direction of the partner
- **Throwing hand:** high and away from the body, fingers on top
- **Back leg:** supporting a majority of the weight (burning sensation in the back leg)
- **Front foot:** closed and up on the toe

On the coach's next verbal command ("throw"), the athletes rock back, step forward, release the baseball, and then hold their follow-through. Check for balance and athleticism, and instruct those who have fallen over to get back on their feet. Then, repeat the drill with the opposite partner starting from the set position, moving to and holding the power position, then throwing and holding the finish.

VARIATIONS

1. *Catch and pop.* Receivers will "pop" to the power position immediately after catching the baseball. The receivers should use two hands and catch the ball out in front of the body. After catching the ball and separating the hands, the receivers quickly shuffle their feet. They should hold the power position and wait for the coach's verbal command to throw. Be sure to use this pop variation when

parents or even an opposing team is watching. It can be really impressive to see 10 to 12 soldiers firing on command and holding that athletic power position.

2. *Long toss competition.* To reward athletes for proper execution in the Broken Throwing drill, you can hold a "long" toss competition. The rules are simple: Partners try to keep the ball from touching the grass (throwing without freezing or stopping). If a pair drops the ball or throws wildly, they are to take a knee and become judges. Start the contest by moving the far throwing line in toward their partners so that they begin 5 feet (152 cm) away from their partner. This ensures that the first toss or two can be made underhand, which helps prevent any pair of players from being out on the first throw. After each throw, the line on the field side should take one to three steps back (more steps for older ages). The athletes continue making throws on the coach's verbal commands until the last pair is left standing—then you have a winner!

COACHING POINTS

1. *Receiving position.* This drill can also be used to work on an athletic receiving stance: feet just outside shoulder width, chest directly facing the thrower, and knees slightly bent. The hands should be held in front of the chest, with the glove held open and the thumbs pointing directly at each other.

2. *Thumbs up or pinkies down.* Put an assistant coach in charge of the receivers, and have athletes work on the thumbs-up and pinkies-down receiving positions.

3. *Get help.* This is another drill where it is beneficial to have lots of help. Give volunteers and assistant coaches a couple baseballs each. Instruct them to stay behind the lines and replace overthrown, underthrown, or otherwise wildly thrown baseballs.

Drill 2 One-Knee Partner Catch

⚾ BEGINNER

EQUIPMENT   Baseball, partner

PURPOSE   This drill removes the legs from the movement so that athletes can focus on the throwing arm and a top-to-bottom path. The arm should follow a full circular path.

PROCEDURE   With athletes in throwing pairs, everyone drops to a knee—the throwing-side knee (right knee for a right-handed thrower). They should place the front foot out in front of the body so that the knee forms a 90-degree angle. Although this may be challenging in itself, the drill is actually just getting started. Start with the baseballs on one side, and have the athletes throw only on a coach's verbal command.

The thrower starts with the hands together, ball held inside the glove. On the coach's call, the athlete takes the ball down and out of the glove before reaching back to the cobra position and then making the throw. After releasing the baseball, the thrower should hold the follow-through. *This* is the focus of the drill (see the photo)—the throwing arm should now be on the opposite side of the front knee (which is at a 90-degree angle in front of the body). The glove should be folded in front of the chest.

Moving from a high power position to this follow-through position (outside of the opposite knee) helps to guide the arm from top to bottom and promotes a full arm circle. The hand moves out of the glove and follows a path that goes down and away. The upper torso rotates so that the front shoulder is closed, now pointing toward the target. After the athletes complete the throw and hold the follow-through position, coaches should check each athlete and help make corrections.

Make sure that no one has teetered over and that the arm did finish across the opposite knee. After you've chased the baseballs down and returned them, the athletes should reverse roles and fire again.

VARIATIONS *Power position freeze.* For a greater challenge, instruct athletes to take a freeze at the power position before throwing. That cobra's fangs should be pointing directly behind the athlete.

COACHING POINTS *Get help.* The learning curve is steep here, and athletes will frequently throw the ball away. If possible, place parents or helpers behind the athletes on both sides. Instruct the athletes NOT to chase the balls and instead let the parents chase them (the parents will be happy to be involved and to get the exercise).

Drill 3 Sprint, Stop, Throw

⚾⚾ INTERMEDIATE

EQUIPMENT One bucket of baseballs, two cones, a catch net or throwing receptacle

PURPOSE This drill involves the feet and teaches athletes to get their body in position when making a throw. The extra movement challenges athletes to make accurate throws under gamelike conditions. Variations can include competitions, points, or unique targets that challenge athletes to perform under pressure as they work on throwing accuracy.

PROCEDURE Start the athletes behind a cone or base, and give each athlete a baseball. On a coach's verbal signal, the first athlete starts to sprint toward a cone placed 15 to 30 feet (4.5 to 9.0 m) in front of the line. Once past the cone, the athlete stops, gathers his momentum, and turns his body to deliver a throw to the target, receptacle, or receiver. Typically, the target is placed on the throwing-arm side of the body (as in the figure, which shows a target for a right-handed thrower). This forces the athlete to move athletically into the power position without spinning or easily pivoting.

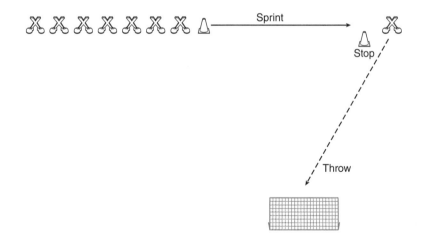

For the first round or two, simply tell athletes to sprint to the cone and make a throw. You'll get a hearty chuckle out of some of the spins, throws, and falling follow-throughs. You'll also be able to prove a point when the athletes' accuracy dramatically improves after they are instructed to slow down, gather their feet, and involve the power position.

VARIATIONS

1. *No stopping cone.* Remove the stopping cone so the athletes don't know when they will be forced to stop and throw. Instead, instruct them to sprint and stop on your verbal command. This simulates a common first-and-third defensive rundown play, for example, where a shortstop or second baseman is running a base runner back from second base toward first base. In this situation, when the runner on third base starts off for home, the infielders yell "four, four!" and the middle infielder must stop, set his feet, and deliver a strike to home plate. Removing the stopping cone simulates the unknown variable of when that runner on third base will take off, and it also increases the degree of difficulty in stopping and shuffling the feet correctly.

2. *Add points.* Increase the energy by including a point reward for accurate throws. If you have a catch net, you can assign points for hitting the bars or making the throw inside the net. See how many points each group can get or how many points a single group can get in a certain time period.

COACHING POINTS

1. *Take your time.* Conduct the drill with a calm demeanor so athletes don't rush their throws. Although the athletes can't move slowly in a game, they need to experience success moving their feet and getting to a good power position before releasing the baseball. Increase the pace later in the season.

2. *Find a fun target.* I've heard of Barry the Bucket, Teddy the Trash Can, and Clyde the Clown as different targets to blast. Although we would all like to toss baseballs at a creepy clown, clowns nowadays can be elusive and difficult to find for youth baseball practices. Instead, take a bucket, draw a face with a big tongue sticking out, and get the kids to knock the tongue off the bucket. You may also come up with other ideas in an effort to keep the kids having fun. Just be sure NOT to count a throw where the athlete does not use the proper footwork.

Drill 4 Reaction Throwing

⚾⚾ INTERMEDIATE

EQUIPMENT   One bucket of baseballs; three catch nets, receptacles, or receivers; disc cones

PURPOSE   This drill enables athletes to work on full-body movements and ground balls when practicing the throwing motion. The drill requires quick reactions, decision making, and throwing accuracy.

PROCEDURE   Place athletes evenly around the infield. With four athletes, for example, place one athlete at third base, one at shortstop, one at second base, and one at first base. With six athletes, simply place three athletes evenly on each side of second base (see figure *a*). Use disc cones to mark their starting positions if necessary. Place a receiver or catch net at third base, home plate, and first base.

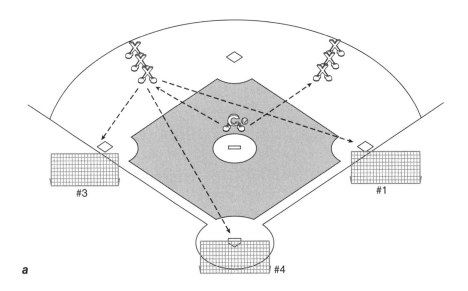

a

Roll or hit ground balls, working your way around the infield. The receiving infielder will have no idea where he is to throw the baseball until the coach yells a number. Just as the ball nears the athlete, choose a receiving target and yell out either "one," "three," or "four." *One* means first base, *three* means third base, and *four* means home plate. Mix up the verbal assignments so athletes make different throws from different angles and different positions. After fielding a ground ball, popping to the power position, and making a throw, athletes should rotate positions so that they work their way around the infield. Include competition and points to increase the energy and fun factor!

VARIATION *Sprint and react.* Move the athletes to a starting line halfway between home plate and first or third base. Place three baseballs in a straight line (3 to 5 feet [90 to 150 cm] apart) directly behind the pitching mound. On a coach's verbal signal, the first athlete sprints toward the baseballs. While the athlete is on the run, the coach yells "right," "center," or "left" to indicate which baseball should be grabbed by the athlete. Then, the coach yells "one," "three," or "four" as the assignment for which base the ball should be thrown to. The coach can stand near the mound and replace the baseballs so that three remain in a line for each athlete to sprint toward. See figure *b*.

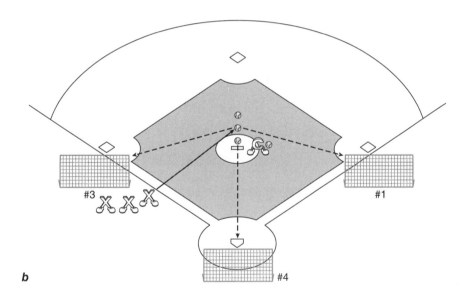

b

COACHING POINTS

1. *Focus on the feet.* With the great unknown comes frantic feet and wild throws. Focus athletes' attention on proper footwork and performing under pressure. For the athlete to make accurate throws, the feet must get into position toward the desired target.

2. *Momentum.* Assign one or two mandatory shuffles that must be performed during the throwing motion. This enables you to include the topic of gathering momentum and gaining power.

Drill 5 Five-Step Throwing Routine

EQUIPMENT   Baseball, partner

PURPOSE   This throwing drill, taught over several sessions, can be done regularly to begin warming up the arms. The routine follows a progression of throwing drills to work through the various movements of a proper throw.

PROCEDURE   This drill includes five steps, which are done one after another. Once again, begin the drill with athletes in pairs along the foul line. Use the following five actions to work on specific movements and incorporate different body parts:

- **Two-knee throwing.** Athletes place both knees on the grass, and their body faces directly at their partner. In one movement, the thrower's shoulders will turn and rotate as the arms extend before releasing and following through.

- **One-knee throwing (see throwing drill 2).** From a one-knee position, athletes turn their torso and get the upper body into the power position. After a two-second hold, the thrower tosses to the receiver and holds the finish for two seconds. The receiver then becomes the thrower and vice versa.

- **Feet in concrete.** For the third movement, the athletes should stand up, but they won't move their feet. Standing and directly facing their target, athletes will turn their shoulders, point the glove, and throw. They should finish by following through with the arm and body, although the feet will not move.

- **Walking step behind.** Now, the athletes should turn sideways with the glove shoulder pointing to their partner. Add a step behind with the back foot. For a right-handed thrower, the right foot would move behind, and step in front of, the left foot. This is followed by a left-foot step, a throw, and a follow-through.

- **Play catch.** Finish by having the athletes play catch normally, and extend the distance between partners as appropriate.

COACHING POINTS   *Introduce each action.* Introduce one or two of the movements at a time. After a little practice, the athletes can follow this routine with little guidance. Although instruction on arm action and the way athletes throw is important, this drill will really assist with the art of playing catch. At each step, the challenge of a different body position helps to hold the athletes' focus. Ahh, there's that word again—*focus.*

The Coach's Clipboard

✔ Remember that patience is a virtue and focus is a learned skill.

✔ Understand both body positioning and arm action and how they work together when executing a throw.

✔ Accept that there are a million different body types and a million different ways to throw.

✔ That being said, teach athletes the throwing absolutes.

✔ Teach the four-seam grip so that athletes learn proper backspin and the straightest flight path possible.

✔ Encourage athletes to use a full follow-through to ensure arm health and to promote moving in the right direction.

✔ Help athletes learn the power position.

✔ Without actively encouraging wild throws, work hard to create an atmosphere where athletes can throw aggressively without fear of making a wild throw.

✔ Include competition at every point possible. Think out of the box to ensure that kids are interested.

✔ Remember to stay positive and be patient. Playing a game of catch is something that former players take for granted.

Developing Pitching Skills With 5 Simple Drills

Beginning pitching is by far the most difficult baseball skill for kids to learn and for coaches to teach. This chapter helps you build a basic level of understanding before putting together a simple plan to follow when teaching the pitching motion. When training young players to pitch, you need to teach pitching in small doses, keeping in mind this analogy: One must bunt before hitting a line drive, and one must bang a double in the gap before smashing a home run.

Yogi Berra once said, "Baseball is 90 percent mental—the other half is physical." This quote couldn't be more appropriate when applied to pitchers. Approach, attitude, and confidence are huge components to successful pitching. The environment that a coach creates at practice and in game situations can have just as much influence on the outcome as the pitcher's physical ability. Therefore, you should stay positive and work slowly. This is all supposed to be fun!

In this chapter, we've provided information on the pitching motion as well as the building blocks of your coaching plan. This information may be applied a year or two down the road of baseball, but it's important to understand where the athletes are heading. Kids will have a difficult enough time playing catch—let alone throwing strikes with a catcher, batter, and umpire. So put a smile on your face, adopt a cool and patient demeanor, and get to work!

Pitching 101

Pitching can be as complex as you want to make it. You can easily confuse a seven-year-old with terms such as *arm slot, release point,* and *flight path.* Likewise, you can keep pitching extremely simple: "Lift your leg, reach back, and let it go!" At the end of the day, a pitcher must simply play catch with that other kid in all the body armor. And just as hitters need to swing hard without thinking about striking out, pitchers need to throw with aggression and pitch without fear. Fear of hitting the batter, fear of walking someone, fear of the coach's wrath—these are pitcher killers, and they are as important for youth coaches to manage as mechanics and fundamentals. That being said, this section on fundamentals first describes the fastball and changeup before moving on to a description of the pitching motion. Consistency comes from solid fundamentals and is the main ingredient in confidence. It's tough to fake confidence, but proper fundamentals are the best way to build up to it.

Pitch Types and Theory

Beginning pitchers should start by working with the four-seam grip for their fastball. From the four-seam grip, an athlete can next learn the two-seam fastball and eventually a changeup. The national youth baseball governing bodies all agree that curveballs can be dangerous for young arms and should be taught by a qualified instructor (ideally taught to an athlete who is postpuberty). Curveballs are not discussed in this book.

Fastball   The fastball is the most basic—yet most important—pitch that an athlete will learn. It is the first pitch that an athlete is taught to throw and remains the number one pitch in his arsenal throughout his career. Not only is the fastball the easiest pitch for a young hurler to throw, but it also helps to strengthen and develop the young arm.

Pitchers use two basic types of fastballs: the four-seam fastball and the two-seam fastball. The four-seam fastball travels straighter and slightly faster than the two-seam fastball, which has more movement (in theory). When introducing these grips, place the priority on throwing strikes. If an athlete is more comfortable and can throw strikes holding the ball with a different grip, by all means, let him use it!

- **Four-seam fastball.** The four-seam fastball grip (figure 6.1) is commonly regarded as the easiest to control and is therefore the first grip taught to a new pitcher. It is formed using the index and middle fingers, the thumb, and the inside of the bent ring finger. The ball is gripped across two of the wide seams (the "horseshoe" or "smile"), with the index and middle fingers resting on top of the stitches ("giving the smile braces"). The thumb is tucked below the ball, resting on or near a bottom seam, and the ring finger and pinkie are curled on the side of the ball. Younger athletes with small hands may feel more comfortable using three fingers across the top of the baseball, and this is fine. However, they should be encouraged to use two fingers as soon as possible. It is called a four-seam fastball because four seams evenly hit the air in front of it when spinning.

Figure 6.1 Four-seam fastball.

• **Two-seam fastball.** Sometimes referred to as a sinker, the two-seam fastball (figure 6.2) moves more than a four-seam fastball and can therefore be slightly more difficult to control. The desired movement is down and in when facing a right-handed batter; the pitch will have a varying

Figure 6.2 Two-seam fastball.

amount of movement depending on the pitcher's unique throwing style.

Just as it sounds, the two-seam fastball is gripped with the index and middle fingers along the two narrow seams ("on the railroad tracks"). Again, the thumb rests directly below the ball, with the inside of the pad resting on an underseam. The ring and pinkie fingers are curled on the side of the ball. For a right-handed pitcher, the two-seam fastball should move both horizontally (to the right) and vertically (down). Therefore, this pitch is commonly thrown to the right-hand side of home plate.

- **Teaching the fastball.** The best type of fastball to teach first is the four-seamer. Whether using two, three, or four fingers on top of the baseball, beginning pitchers find this pitch easier to control, and throwing it helps them build arm strength. The idea of "pitching by the book" calls for throwing a two-seam fastball to the right side of the plate (inside to a right-handed hitter) and throwing a four-seam fastball to the left side of the plate. Understanding these by-the-book tendencies, you should put your focus back on strikes and do whatever you can to help your pitchers throw them.

Changeup Regardless of how hard a pitcher throws, hitters will eventually catch up to a fastball. As a pitcher advances into high school, college, and beyond, changing speeds is absolutely necessary for success. And for beginning pitchers, it can be a fun and effective way to mix things up. The changeup, thrown with the same arm action and release as a fastball, is the first of these off-speed pitches. The changeup is a deception pitch intended to disrupt a hitter's timing and rhythm—it's designed to fool the batter (which is different than beating a batter with crazy movement). The unique grip of the changeup results in less velocity and subsequently more movement than with a fastball. Because the palm faces home plate and there is little wrist movement, the changeup is safe and can be taught at an early age.

The purpose of the changeup is to make the batter *think* that he sees a fastball. Because the batter times his swing to the pace of a fastball, he will swing before the pitch has entered the strike zone. Now out in front of the pitch, the batter will either slow his bat down to make contact or swing and miss altogether. When teaching the changeup, the most important point to emphasize is to maintain full arm speed. A changeup fools batters because the pitch is thrown with an arm speed, delivery, and release that are nearly identical to those for a fastball. *Pitchers should not slow down their arms when throwing a changeup.* Instead, they should have confidence that the changeup grip will ensure that the pitch comes out with less velocity than a fastball (off speed!). Additionally, young pitchers should be steered away from accelerating their windup in an effort to make the batter think they are going to throw a super-fast fastball, only to slow down and release an arching moon ball. Although this can actually work against hitters who are seeing live pitching for the first time, it won't work for long and is a sure giveaway for ages 10 and above.

The most important ingredient in the success of a changeup is speed—it should be 8 to 12 miles per hour slower than a pitcher's fastball. Treat movement as a total bonus, and allow it to happen naturally.

- **Three-finger changeup.**
The three-finger grip (figure 6.3) is the easiest to control, regardless of the size of a pitcher's hand. The first three fingers (index, middle, and ring) are placed on top of the ball and spread out evenly. Both the thumb and the pinkie are in contact with the ball, tucked underneath. For the changeup, the ball is held farther back in the hand—away from the finger-tips—than for the fastball grip, in a position that is called "choking" the ball. The ball is pressed firmly back into the pads of the open

Figure 6.3 Three-finger changeup.

hand; care is taken to avoid pressing the ball directly against the palm. (The pads help maintain touch with the off-speed pitch.) There should be space between the bottom of the palm and the baseball, and the fingers on top of the ball should be well spread out.

If the pitcher starts with a fastball grip, the fastball fingers (power fingers) move to the inside of the ball, taking velocity off of the pitch. The index finger moves to the inside of the baseball, the middle finger moves to the top of the baseball, and the ring finger moves to the outside of the baseball (up from underneath the baseball). The three-finger changeup grip is an easy adjustment from either the four-seam or two-seam fastball grip. When the changeup is thrown from a four-seam grip, the three-finger change has a long seam (the side of the "horseshoe") pressing directly into the pads of the hand, and the three power fingers all reach across the opposite seam. When it is thrown off of a two-seam grip, the fingers are evenly distributed around the "railroad tracks." Looking down at the three-finger change across a two-seam grip, the pitcher should see, from right to left, the ring finger, seam, middle finger, seam, and index finger.

The three-finger changeup can be used to encourage athletes to use two fingers on top of a fastball. Tell your pitchers that you'll teach them the changeup just as soon as they show you they can throw a fastball with two fingers. It's amazing what athletes can do when you challenge them!

• **Four-finger (or circle) changeup.** The circle change (figure 6.4) is a sexy pitch that every young pitcher wants to throw. As a pitcher matures and the size of his hand increases, he may need to take more velocity off of his three-finger changeup. The grip for the circle change is a natural next step from the three-finger grip; it is reached by moving the power fingers even farther inside the baseball. To review, the index and middle fingers move inside the baseball on a three-finger change so that the index finger is

Figure 6.4　Four-finger (circle) changeup.

on the inside of the ball and the middle finger is directly on top. The ring finger moves up from underneath the baseball and lies on the outside of the ball. In essence, the power fingers have moved inside the baseball one "click" in an effort to turn down the velocity of the pitch.

The circle change grip is reached by moving inside the baseball another click or by turning down the power once again. It is called a circle change because the index finger moves completely to the inside of the baseball and may form a circle by connecting to the thumb. The middle finger moves inside the baseball, while the ring finger moves up near the top of the baseball. Even the pinkie adjusts, moving up along the baseball so that it now rests on the outside of the baseball. The coach's verbal cue to help the pitcher with this grip is "Inside, seam, seam, outside." This cue summarizes what the pitcher sees as he looks down at the grip for a circle changeup across a two-seam position:

- The index finger is inside the baseball, or closest to the body or head during release.
- The middle finger rests along a seam.
- The ring finger rests along the other seam.
- The pinkie is outside the baseball.

Because the power fingers are so far inside the baseball, the velocity of the circle change should be less than that of a three-finger changeup, and the movement should increase down and away from a left-handed hitter.

- **Teaching the changeup.** The key to a changeup is keeping the arm motion, arm angle, and release as similar as possible to those of the fastball delivery. "Set the changeup grip, and think *fastball!*" is good advice. Because the power fingers (index and middle) have moved inside the baseball, there will naturally be much less velocity than on a fastball. Encourage the athlete to throw his changeup—as much as possible—the way he throws his fastball. The athlete needs to trust the grip to slow the ball down. Give the pitcher encouragement such as "Don't think too much . . . just throw it!"

Start by teaching the three-finger grip and then move to the circle change as necessary for either increased movement or decreased velocity. Because the arm action on a changeup is very similar to that on a fastball, there are no real age restrictions on when to learn and throw the pitch. Throwing a changeup does not increase the chance for physical injury. However, a young pitcher's first goal is to develop and master the fastball. Even though this may come at the expense of some hits and runs, a pitcher must be comfortable with the fastball and must be able to repeat the pitching motion before learning and incorporating a changeup.

Mechanics and the Pitching Motion

Pitchers use two methods to deliver a baseball. The first, called the *windup,* is the full-motion whirlybird delivery that starts with the pitcher's chest facing home plate; the pitcher's first movement is a step back behind the rubber. This style of pitching is used with no one on base or with no base runners in position to steal a base. The second way of pitching, called the *stretch,* starts with the pitcher in a sideways position; the pitcher's movement begins with a leg lift. Because this stretch motion is much shorter and quicker to the plate, it is used when base runners are in a position where they may steal.

Here's some good news: In youth baseball, base runners can't lead off and can't steal until about the 9- or 10-year-old age group. Trust me, this is a huge responsibility *off* of a coach's clipboard. And this also means that a pitcher can use either the windup or stretch motion while learning to pitch. For these early baseball years, although you have the flexibility to allow an athlete to mimic the big leaguer he saw on TV last night, you just shouldn't do it! The recommended strategy is to start teaching pitchers from the stretch motion first. The stretch is short and simple, and it minimizes the degree of difficulty associated with throwing strikes. Fewer body parts and fewer movements equal more strikes.

Stretch Motion

The stretch motion is broken down into three simple steps that are easy to teach and easy to follow. Communicate this simple number system and use its similarity to the hitting technique described in chapter 7 to create an easy-to-follow instruction plan.

- **Stance.** The stretch stance (figure 6.5*a*) is formed by placing the back foot directly next to the pitcher's rubber (that white rectangular thing in the middle of the mound). The front foot is positioned about 6 inches (15 cm) away, parallel to the back foot (looks like a pair of skis). The hands are held high in front of the chest, and the eyes are locked in on the catcher.

- **Position 1—Leg lift.** The first thing the athlete does is lift the front leg. There is no step back, no load or twist, just a simple leg lift. At the peak of the leg lift is the balance point, which is the position where the lift leg forms a right angle. Position 1 (figure 6.5*b*) requires balance and stability to keep the body posture tall, the foot out, and the toe pointing down.

- **Position 2—Power position.** From the leg lift position, the glove, throwing hand, and lift leg move together to the power position (figure 6.5*c*). Perhaps the most important key here is that a majority of the athlete's weight should remain over the back leg as the limbs move. Once the athlete is at position 2, the glove arm is extended toward home plate, the throwing hand points back toward second base, and the front foot has reached out toward home plate (with the side of the shoe pointing toward home plate). It looks like a big X, and the goal is for the pitcher to be in a comfortable, athletic position. This is called a loaded throwing position because the body's weight has been held back, and it is very similar to the stride and load position in hitting technique (hitting position 1). If the athletes do this correctly, you are sure to hear some groans about burning leg and shoulder muscles.

- **Position 3—Finish.** Once an athlete has reached the loaded power position, the next move is an explosion toward home plate and an aggressive delivery (figure 6.5*d*). A number is not assigned to the release point because we want this to be physical and aggressive—no thinking. To be technical, the body is supposed to finish with
  - the front foot pointing directly to home plate;
  - the trail leg even with the front foot, with the knee in and the toe pointing down;
  - the glove arm folded in front of the chest; and
  - the throwing arm down by the opposite knee.

Figure 6.5 The stretch motion: *(a)* the stance, *(b)* leg lift, *(c)* power position, and *(d)* finish.

The upper body should follow through so that the back is just about flat, parallel to the ground. Again, the goal is to teach a comfortable and athletic position where the body has supported the throwing arm and has left the athlete in a position to field any ground balls or line drives.

Windup Motion

The windup begins with the pitcher directly facing home plate. The feet are once again roughly shoulder-width apart, the hands are high in front of the chest, and the eyes are locked on the target. The only difference between the stretch and the windup motions is two small steps: right and left. For a right-handed pitcher, the first movement is a step back and at an angle with the left leg (see figure 6.6a). Next, the athlete performs a small lift of the right leg before turning it open and placing it down right next to and directly parallel to the pitching rubber (see figure 6.6b). From this position, it's a simple 1, 2, and 3! The finish position is shown in figure 6.6c.

Figure 6.6 Windup motion: *(a)* step back, *(b)* lift and pivot, and *(c)* finish position.

Coaching Beginning Pitchers

Coaching pitchers is completely different than knowing how to pitch. As mentioned before, you should start with the stretch motion and add the windup steps later. Follow a similar instruction plan as with hitting (see chapter 7): a simple number system to identify the major points of instruction. But move slowly and make sure the pitchers are having fun and throwing hard! Use the following checkpoints and include one or two in each practice in the specified order:

- **Teach throwing first.** Use the basics covered in chapter 5 to teach the basic fundamentals of throwing a baseball. If an athlete can't hit the side of a barn when playing catch, a leg lift and power position may not do much to help him.

- **Teach the stretch stance.** In the stretch stance, the feet are under the armpits (like a pair of skis), the hands are high and in front of the chest, and the eyes are on the target. The windup presents multiple steps, body turns, and much more motion in general. Teach the stretch stance position and then allow the athlete to get comfortable letting it rip. Help the athlete get comfortable in the stretch position, using the proper starting stance. At this point, limit the instruction to "Lift your leg and let it rip."

- **Add rules for position 1.** Whether you're coaching a group or an individual, the first fundamental to add is the leg lift. Include a hold or freeze at the balance point, and teach these rules:
  - The foot should be out under the knee (lift leg).
  - The toes should be pointing down (lift leg).
  - The body should be tall with solid balance.

A pitcher should be able to collect himself and balance at position 1 during practice, although he should never stop during a game. Hypothetically, stopping will break momentum and could decrease velocity. But for fundamental practice, freezing at position 1 slows the body down and helps to prevent a rushed or hurried delivery. Always finish practice by having the athletes throw at full speed, but at this point, push hard for proper technique.

- **Add rules for position 3.** Next, you should add instruction on the finish—without causing the athletes to lose aggression or think too much about the delivery. The finish should be strong and balanced with the feet roughly straight across, the glove in front of the chest, and the throwing shoulder over the landing knee. If focusing on the finish throws your athlete out of whack, back off and keep him going hard.

Details

Before you move on to more details, your athlete should be able to lift his leg under control (position 1), reach back and throw the ball with aggression, and control some semblance of a finish (position 3)—and do all of this without falling over. Having accomplished these checkpoints, this athlete should be throwing strikes. Moving forward, you can address more detailed issues such as the following:

- **Rules for position 2.** The biggest fundamental key to teaching position 2 is to get the athlete to keep his weight back and *load.* With the athlete holding a freeze at position 2, you should look for these keys:
  - The throwing arm should be reaching back toward second base.
  - The glove arm should be reaching out toward home plate.
  - The front foot should be extended toward home plate (closed at this point).
  - The weight should be loaded on the back leg (slight bend in the back leg).
- **Alignment (direction).** Where is the lead leg landing? Chances are it is stepping way open (toward first base for a right-hander). If so, this needs to be corrected. Similar to a car, the alignment is off—and similar to a mechanic, you need to fix it!
- **Stride length (distance).** Assuming that the lead leg is now moving in the general direction of home plate, you can help the athlete work on extending the stride length. Referred to as a surge, this is the *explode* that needs to follow the *load* at position 2.
- **Windup.** Pitchers will be excited to learn the windup, but you should keep an eye out for super-speed deliveries.
- **Changeup.** The fastball fingers must be on the inside of the baseball at release. If they are behind the ball, the speed will be too fast. Use the grip to help young athletes easily stay inside. They should throw it hard so that the batter has a chance to be fooled!

Here is the pitching coach's goal: Get an athlete to take a leg lift (position 1) with strength and balance, unleash an aggressive and full fastball, and finish under control with a strong and balanced follow-through (position 3). If a pitcher can do this, there is a good chance that the pitcher will be around the strike zone. A more athletic youngster will throw more strikes than the player who is less coordinated. However, ALL athletes *can* execute position 1 and 3 while throwing hard, and this is the key to throwing strikes!

Basic Tips for Coaching Pitching

Here are some basic tips for coaching pitching. Keep these in mind and your pitchers will love you.

- **Provide opportunities for success.** In practice, find an enclosed bullpen area where wild throws can be contained. Keep your pitcher focused on learning positions and movements without worrying about throwing balls or strikes. In games, search for opportunities where athletes have the best chance for success. Start new pitchers with a fresh inning and no runners on base. If this pitcher is fragile, try to find a situation with a lop-sided score (e.g., up by 8 or down by 10).

- **Rotate pitchers.** Your job is about developing your kids. Work as many kids through the mound as possible. Similar to position players screaming to play shortstop or first base, most athletes will want to pitch. Simple rules such as "infield to outfield and outfield to infield" encourage movement of athletes between positions. All kids should be given the opportunity to pitch at some point! You may need to find a 10-1 or 1-10 lopsided score to get that 10th, 11th, and 12th kid onto the mound, but in the end the development is worth it.

- **Encourage pitchers to throw strikes.** Defensive support is rarely found in beginning baseball games. But pitchers must be encouraged to throw strikes and get batters to hit the ball. Walks give your team no chance of getting outs, so batted balls should be celebrated!

- **Promote a DWI (Deal With It) mentality.** To put it in plainer language—*no complaining*! Baseball, a game of failure, involves lots of adversity. Pitching, in particular, is a position that requires thick skin. Establish a no-complaining rule and work hard to assist pitchers to deal with it (DWI mentality).

- **Maintain your big-picture focus.** Here are some things to remember: Monitor pitch counts and don't overuse your pitchers. Develop as many athletes on the mound as possible, and find times to let all interested pitchers toe the rubber. Keep things fun and work hard to stay positive. Every pitcher will be pulled off the mound at some point during the season, and your character-building skills will be tested.

Drill 1 Group Freeze Drills

⊘BEGINNER

EQUIPMENT   Baseballs (optional), a backstop or catch nets (if available)

PURPOSE   This drill is used to teach multiple athletes the body mechanics of pitching.

PROCEDURE   Line the athletes up, parallel to one another, along a foul line or at individual pitching rubbers. Use bullpens with multiple mounds if available. Following the instructional order described earlier in this chapter, teach the athletes pitching fundamentals and include freezing and holding at specific positions.

The first fundamental to teach is the stretch stance. The athletes should be standing side by side, with room to flail and flop. Teach the athletes to assume the position: feet like skis (back foot against the rubber), hands high in front of the chest, and eyes on a target. As a coach, you have a clean view of all the athletes in front of you and can make corrections as necessary. If baseballs and some sort of catch net are available, instruct the pitchers to lift their leg and throw after they properly show the stretch position.

Follow the same line of thinking to teach position 1. On your verbal command, athletes should assume the stretch position, putting the right foot in front of the left and removing fingers from noses. Then use a simple verbal command of "number one" to instruct the athletes to move to the balance point. After they hold this position for two to three seconds, follow with a "throw" or "fire" command and let the athletes pitch.

Based on the recommended instructional order, you will train position 3 (finish) next. Lifeletics trains under the assumption that strikes come from a controlled start, an aggressive throw, and a balanced follow-through or finish. The same holds true for the baseball swing. But for pitching, you should introduce the stance, position 1, and position 3—and then have fun getting involved with position 2 (power position).

COACHING POINTS

1. *Athlete keywords.* The kids respond well to a verbal keyword. At each position, have the athletes themselves yell a different keyword to assist with remembering each position:

   - Position 1—balance!
   - Position 2—power!
   - Position 3—finish!

   These athletes may not remember that a proper leg lift has the foot out and the toe down, but they will go home and show their parents when they are supposed to yell, "Balance!"

2. *Finish with rhythm.* As with most baseball techniques, you should finish each session by allowing the athletes to move through the motion without stopping. The most important rule is that the athletes should throw hard! Encourage and guide proper mechanics while the kids let that baseball fly!

Drill 2 Bullpen Buddies

EQUIPMENT   Baseball, hitter with helmet, catcher with gear

PURPOSE   This drill accomplishes multiple goals while athletes are practicing pitching. First, it builds arm strength and stamina because pitchers throw 20 to 40 pitches. Second, it works to remove fear of pitching with a batter standing in the box. Finally, Bullpen Buddies helps hitters to increase their own comfort with baseballs being pitched at them.

PROCEDURE   Kid-pitch is a new and scary phenomenon for young baseball players. Bullpen Buddies is nothing more than a live pitching session with catcher and batter. This type of session is called a bullpen. Pitchers go to a designated area and follow a throwing routine to practice their motion, build up their pitch counts, and work on mound presence. As batting practice is to a hitter, a bullpen is to a pitcher.

Bullpen Buddies requires a batter (with bat and helmet) to stand in the batter's box while the pitcher throws his bullpen. Include this drill during batting practice and rotate a hitter through the bullpen area as one of the batting stations. Game conditions are best simulated if a catcher in gear is also involved, but the hitter is never allowed to swing.

VARIATIONS   *Freeze drills.* During any bullpen session, freeze drills can help to develop strength, balance, and command of the pitching motion. Have the pitcher freeze at position 1 to work on the balance point. Have the pitcher freeze at position 2 to work on keeping the weight back and loading the back leg. Have the pitcher freeze at position 3 to work on firming up the landing leg and getting into a good fielding position.

COACHING POINTS

1. *Hitters with gloves.* If your athletes are just starting kid-pitch, batters can stand in wearing a glove instead of wielding a bat. Both batter and pitcher now know that a hit batsman can be avoided.

2. *Have fun.* Everyone is scared during Bullpen Buddies. Hitters are afraid of getting hit, pitchers are afraid of hitting someone . . . heck, the catcher is likely scared of a ball in the dirt. You may even experience sweaty palms when you witness close calls and near misses. Allow the batter to back off the plate until comfortable. Allow the pitcher to throw outside fastballs until comfortable. Do what it takes to let these kids get used to live pitchers and hitters.

Drill 3 Chair Drills

EQUIPMENT   Chair (or bucket), baseball, towel, partner (for the variation)

PURPOSE   These drills can be used to train pitching fundamentals with a fun prop. The Towel Snap drill helps the athlete align the body and put the pitching motion in rhythm. It teaches extension and release point out in front, while making sure that the body's balance, rhythm, and timing are smooth. The Superman Finish drill teaches the athlete to firm up the front leg and control the body's weight through the follow-through. Most important, these drills allow for multiple repetitions in a short amount of time, and they don't require throwing a live baseball.

PROCEDURE

- **Towel snap drill.** Place a chair in a position down the mound, directly in front of the pitcher in between the rubber and home plate. Holding a towel, the athlete goes through the pitching motion and attempts to smack the seat of the chair with the towel (see photo *a*). If done correctly, there should be a loud snap when the towel strikes the chair. This happens when the body works together and the release point is well out in front of the body. If the release point is back—farther behind the body— then the towel will gently flop against the chair or even miss it altogether. The chair should be far enough away that a pitcher will have to extend his reach to touch the chair with a towel. Technically, a pitcher's stride

(continued)

length should be 90 to 100 percent of his height. The chair should also extend a foot or two for the length of the athlete's arm and the towel he's holding. However, be careful not to place the chair beyond an athlete's natural reach. If no chairs are readily available, you can stand in front of the pitcher and hold out your own glove as a towel target. Just be careful to avoid the whip end of that towel—it hurts!

• **Superman finish drill.** Place a chair directly over the pitching rubber, and ask the pitcher to place his back foot on the chair (see photo *b*). The pitcher should rest the back foot so that the inside of the ankle faces down and the hips remain closed to home plate. The front foot is extended toward home plate (have the pitcher close the foot slightly if he needs help holding his balance). Holding a baseball with his hands together in front of his chest, the athlete rocks back and fires toward the glove or catch net. The back foot will turn over so that the laces face down, showing that the hips have exploded. However, the back foot must not leave the chair. The throwing arm will finish across the body so that the throwing shoulder lines up over the landing knee with the glove high and in front of the chest. The athlete's body weight is forced to finish (correctly) centered over the landing leg as the hips rotate, and the back leg turns over but does NOT leave the chair. The flat-back position here is called

a Superman finish, and athletes are challenged to "fly straight" and hold their balance. In this drill, a top-to-bottom delivery is ensured because the trail leg is removed from the movement. By taking away the trail leg, the Superman Finish drill encourages a pitcher to firm up and move directly through the lead leg. The drill also provides a number of teaching points with regard to the finish position: weight distribution (through the landing leg), a flat back (Superman finish), the glove arm in front of the chest, and the throwing shoulder over the landing knee. Finally, the drill helps build leg strength in the landing leg. In this drill, young athletes realize just how important leg strength is to pitching successfully.

VARIATION *Partner towel drill.* Instead of using a chair, have an athlete stand in front of his partner and hold out his glove. The "throwing" partner uses the towel to smack his partner's glove. Warn the partners to be sure to step back and avoid being whacked themselves!

COACHING POINTS *Avoid the crutch.* The Superman Finish drill helps athletes who fall heavily on their trail leg. Typically, this means a rotational, side-to-side delivery. Without even understanding these fundamentals, an athlete will respond to the challenge of holding his balance after throwing now that the crutch has been removed (back leg stays on the chair). This is a good way to provide advanced pitching instruction that is both fun and challenging!

Drill 4 Homework—Individual Freeze Drills

⚾⚾ INTERMEDIATE

EQUIPMENT   Mirror or reflective surface, consistent effort

PURPOSE   This drill helps athletes learn pitching fundamentals through regular practice.

PROCEDURE   Assign homework for athletes to do in between practices. These freeze drills should be done in front of a mirror and ideally with a parent's participation. Depending on where the athlete is at in the learning process, homework assignments can involve freeze drills at position 1, 2, or 3. Additionally, freeze drills can involve multiple positions (1 and 3, 2 and 3, or even a combination such as 2-1-3).

- **Freeze at position 1—balance point.** The athlete performs a three-second hold at the leg lift or balance point (see photo *a*). The goal is for the athlete to have a tall and proud body posture while holding steady before finishing the motion. Pitchers must stay in control of their own body!

- **Freeze at position 2—power position.** The athlete should work on keeping the weight back as he loads the back leg (see photo *b*). Moving from the balance point to position 2, the athlete should arrive at the power position with the majority of his weight over the back leg. Have the athlete lift the front toe to show that his weight is back. With the athlete in this loaded position 2, issue the command to "rock back and fire!" The athlete goes from *load* to *explode* toward the target.

a   b   c

- **Freeze at position 3—finish position.** Holding a firm finish ensures that the front (landing) leg firms up, stopping the body's forward momentum and transferring all power and momentum into the throwing arm (see photo *c*). Assign a three-second hold at the finish position, and have the athlete correct his posture and positioning appropriately.

VARIATION *Combination work.* Include stops and starts, moving forward and back. A challenging assignment is a 2-1-3: The athlete moves from the stance through the leg lift and freezes for three seconds at position 2. Then, the athlete moves backward to the balance point (position 1) and holds for three seconds. Leaving the leg lift position, the athlete loads the back leg and explodes forward to position 3 (holding the finish for three seconds).

COACHING POINTS *Get parents involved.* Kids don't like homework, no matter how you disguise it. Communicate to the parents what you want done in between practices and put the accountability on them to do the work. If the parents can learn the positions and details of each fundamental number, then the athlete's development will undoubtedly happen faster.

Drill 5 Pitchers Fielding Practice (PFPs)

EQUIPMENT   Infield diamond or throw-down bases, athletes at infield positions, coach with baseballs

PURPOSE   PFPs teach pitchers to field their position by allowing them to practice a series of plays most commonly experienced by pitchers.

PROCEDURE   Place infielders at their positions and a single pitcher on the mound (other pitchers can wait off of the diamond or at other positions). Walk through a routine of four ground-ball situations:

1. **Comebacker.** After the pitcher releases a pitch or goes through a delivery without a baseball, the coach hits or throws a ground ball back at the pitcher. Pitchers field, get a four-seam grip, and fire to first base (see figure *a*). Involve the infielders here by simulating a runner on first; the comebacker now starts a double play (1-6-3).

2. **Bunt.** Roll a bunt to one side of the pitching mound (see figure *b*). Emphasize proper footwork and fielding fundamentals.

3. **1-2-3—comebacker with bases loaded.** The pitcher fields the ball and fires it to the catcher. The catcher then fires to first to complete the double play (see figure *c*).

4. **Covering first base on ground ball to right side.** The pitcher works on covering first base on a ground ball to the right side of the infield (see figure *d*).

VARIATION   *Add runners.* If you really want to challenge your pitchers and defense, add live base runners to the drill. And if you have the guts, stand in the batter's box and have your pitcher throw a pitch before each ground ball that you throw or hit.

COACHING POINTS   *Teach first, drill second.* PFPs require some sort of familiarity with the plays involved. Both infielders and pitchers need to be introduced to these situations and their respective defensive plays.

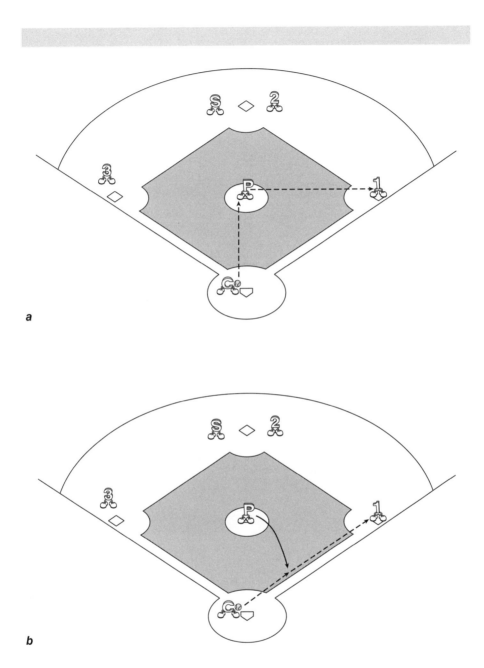

a

b

(continued)

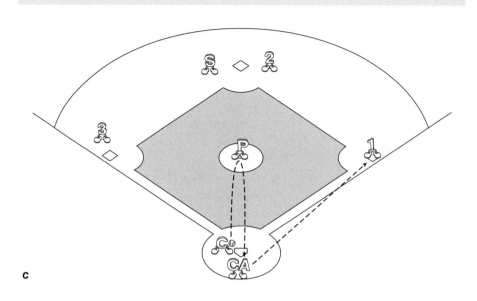

c

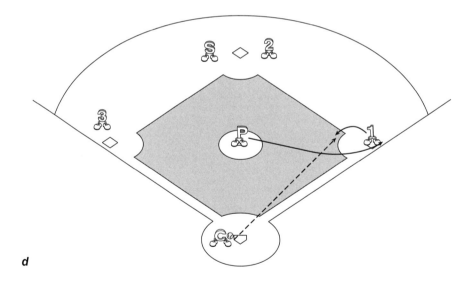

d

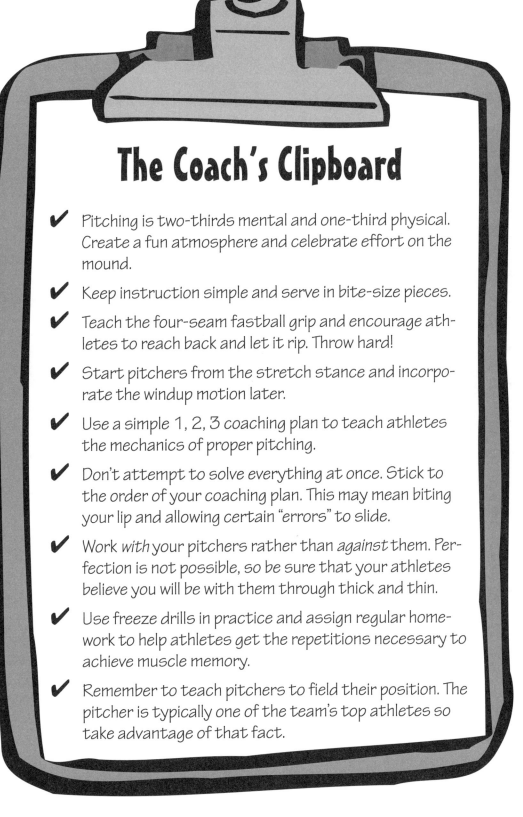

The Coach's Clipboard

✔ Pitching is two-thirds mental and one-third physical. Create a fun atmosphere and celebrate effort on the mound.

✔ Keep instruction simple and serve in bite-size pieces.

✔ Teach the four-seam fastball grip and encourage athletes to reach back and let it rip. Throw hard!

✔ Start pitchers from the stretch stance and incorporate the windup motion later.

✔ Use a simple 1, 2, 3 coaching plan to teach athletes the mechanics of proper pitching.

✔ Don't attempt to solve everything at once. Stick to the order of your coaching plan. This may mean biting your lip and allowing certain "errors" to slide.

✔ Work *with* your pitchers rather than *against* them. Perfection is not possible, so be sure that your athletes believe you will be with them through thick and thin.

✔ Use freeze drills in practice and assign regular homework to help athletes get the repetitions necessary to achieve muscle memory.

✔ Remember to teach pitchers to field their position. The pitcher is typically one of the team's top athletes so take advantage of that fact.

Developing Hitting Skills With 5 Simple Drills

Throughout this book, we've emphasized that coaches should teach the fundamentals first—and then teach a *realistic application* of those fundamentals. When it comes to working with beginning baseball players, teaching hitting is waaaaaaaay different than knowing how to hit. If you can get an athlete to set his feet, pound the plate, and take a stance . . . then make a full and aggressive swing without falling down . . . you, my friend, are an excellent youth baseball coach. You do not need to be a hitting expert to have a profoundly positive impact on a young batter. With a simple plan and some minor adjustments, the majority of hitters can quickly morph from spinning tops to well-oiled hitting machines.

Teaching hitting is one of the easiest and most fulfilling tasks of the youth baseball coach. There's nothing better than watching confidence grow as the ball starts jumping off of an athlete's bat. Lots of the basic instruction can be covered in group formats, where the athletes each grab a bat and then spread out in front of you. But remember that there is a time for teaching and a time for swings. Incorporating both *instruction* (teaching athletes how to swing the bat correctly) and *batting practice* (getting athletes swings) is important for the athletes' development.

Follow a simple plan with young hitters and you'll find that most parents will come to view you as a great hitting coach.

To provide effective instruction on hitting, you need to have a basic understanding of the swing—as well as how to teach that swing. When it's time for BP, the themes from earlier chapters hold true: Get the athletes into as many small groups as possible, and focus on allowing them to get swings!

Hitting 101

The batting swing can be broken down into four positions: stance, load (position 1), contact (position 2), and finish (position 3). These four components can be found in every swing, although sometimes you might have to look pretty closely to find them. All joking aside, if you can successfully teach these basic positions to your athletes, you give them the foundation they need in order to develop their swings over time. For example, without the ability to keep the feet under control, an athlete will find it nearly impossible to control the arms and hands during a swing. Give your players the chance to learn. Work hard and be diligent to learn the four positions of the swing.

Stance

The proper stance should be athletic and comfortable (figure 7.1). Although athletes are required to wear a helmet at all times, it is not necessary to have two batting gloves, three wristbands, sunglasses, and body armor. Different athletes will have different swings, but they can all use this basic stance to establish a hitting plan:

- The feet are positioned outside of shoulder width, and the knees are slightly bent.
- The hands are held comfortably in front of the back shoulder.
- The head and eyes are focused on the direction of the baseball (the pitcher or wherever the baseball is coming from).
- For the grip, the dominant hand is on top (right hand for right-handed batter, left hand for left-handed batter); the hands are connected and just up from the bottom knob of the bat. The batter should line up the first or second knuckles and squeeze the bat firmly—but shouldn't kill it! (See drill 2 in this chapter for a tip on teaching the athletes to find the proper grip.)

Figure 7.1 *(a)* Proper batting stance, and *(b)* grip.

Position 1—Stride and Load

Just before a batter takes a swing, the body generates momentum and power by "loading." This is nothing more than a short step forward in combination with a small movement of the hands backward. It closely resembles the loaded *power position* used during throwing (see chapter 5). The head and body remain pretty still during the movement from stance to load (figure 7.2).

- The front foot steps 4 to 6 inches (10 to 15 cm) forward, landing softly to keep the body balanced and the head still.

- The hands shift 2 to 3 inches (5 to 7.5 cm) back, away from the body.

Figure 7.2 Stride and load.

Position 2—Contact

The contact position (figure 7.3) is something that you'll teach later, but you should understand it now. Understanding the nuts and bolts of making proper contact could just make you the hero of your own slowpitch softball game. Impress your buddies by driving the softball with power and grace, instead of buying a round after another whiff!

Figure 7.3 Contact.

The contact position is where the bat meets the ball—or where the bat *should* meet the ball. Fortunately, when kids are learning how to play baseball, the ball is initially placed on a tee and doesn't move. This can help quite a bit, allowing both coach and athlete to focus on finding the barrel of the bat. Whether an athlete's swing resembles Ted Williams' swing or something out of a bloopers video, the goal is to make consistent contact and to do so without falling over.

Technically, here are the details of position 2:

- The bat should contact the ball when it is even with the inside of the front foot, something to keep in mind if working with a tee.
- The position of the upper body should be as follows:
  - The bottom arm is extended with the palm facing down.
  - The top arm is slightly bent, forming an L shape, with the palm facing up.
  - The chin starts at the left shoulder and finishes on the right shoulder.
- The lower body should do the following:

- The hips rotate; the back foot spins or rotates on the ball of the foot so that the back knee turns inward toward the front knee. This action is commonly referred to as "squishing the bug"—a reference to stepping on a spider and squashing it into the ground.
- The front leg starts to firm up at contact (not much swaying movement forward).
- The batter should have a balanced and strong body position with slightly more weight on the back leg than the front leg.

Position 3—Finish

Hitters should be challenged to take an aggressive swing without falling over (figure 7.4). Getting athletes to do this is goal number one for the youth baseball coach when teaching hitting. Use the Three-Step Hitting drill (page 120) to get hitters to focus on properly holding a finish position after swinging the bat. But always make sure that they swing the stinkin' bat. Hitters should be hitters, not walkers or lookers!

Here are the nuts and bolts of position 3:

- The front leg is firm, with the foot slightly closed.

Figure 7.4 Finish.

- The back foot has turned completely inward—that stinking bug has been annihilated!
- The hands follow through and finish above the front shoulder (two hands on the bat).
- The head and eyes look down at the point of contact (the head rests on the right shoulder for a right-handed batter).
- The finish is balanced and strong!

Teaching Hitting

To quote that wise man once again, "If you can teach an athlete to find a batting stance, take an aggressive swing, and *not* fall over, you are a good youth baseball coach." You must leave the nuances of the hands and arms to the athlete until you have taught a proper stance, load, and finish. This means the order of instruction follows a predetermined sequence:

1. Stance
2. Stride and load
3. Finish
4. Details

Use the information in this section to ensure that you have a time and place for teaching and a time and place for simply letting the athletes get swings. Select a single position of the swing to cover in a specific practice, and work the athletes through the swing over time. Group work is encouraged; have the athletes form a line or circle with plenty of room for swings. Young hitters are often hesitant to ask questions. When they can look left or right at the athlete next to them, it can be a big help.

Incorporating Hitting Into a Practice Plan

The use of station instruction and multiple groups is especially important when it comes to practicing hitting. Think of how many swings each athlete takes during a given practice, and try to maximize that number. Do not get caught running the typical Little League practice where a coach stands on the mound, 46-plus feet away from home plate, reliving his glory days by trying to fire strikes to a single batter at home plate. The rest of the team ends up standing in the outfield picking grass and digging holes while the batter grows frustrated at the lack of strikes to swing at. In the end, the batter ends up swinging at more balls than strikes, while the rest of the team recites the "this is boring" anthem.

Instead, break the team into small groups and use as many stations as possible. Use your helpers and get athletes swings! Remember, coaches and parents don't have to be hitting experts to place a ball on a tee or toss a wiffle ball. Although hitting on the field is something that is fun for athletes, you should also have two or three other stations where swings can be taken quickly and consistently. To achieve this, use any bullpen areas, foul territory, or open patches of grass. Involve catch nets, wiffle balls, and tennis balls to minimize cleanup time. Keep stations quick (7 to 10 minutes) to maximize the number of swings taken by each athlete.

Batting practice stations can be designed for repetition (swings), execution (bunting, hit-and-run, and so on), or instruction (training) (see figure 7.5). Include competition and fun to mask the "work" of hitting. Get creative to maximize space, and use tee work, wiffle balls, or stationary hitting devices where field space is limited. Remember to celebrate success and keep athletes smiling; hitting is tough and takes time to learn.

This type of station instruction and batting practice gives you the opportunity to teach. Even if you are not a hitting expert, you can at least teach stance, load, and finish—or someone on your coaching staff can. By breaking the team into groups and rotating the groups through a number of stations, you can have a single station that is dedicated to instruction. And if you're not comfortable teaching hitting yet, focus each station on getting the kids swings . . . and reread this chapter!

Figure 7.5   Sample Batting Practice Stations

Station	Activity or drill
1	Instruction Soft Toss (Bullpen Area) Three-Step Hitting drill—wide stance (no stride)
2	Wiffle Balls (Foul Territory)—live swings
3	Tennis Ball Drill (Right-Field Line)—stride and turn in (overcome fear of getting hit)
4	Tee Work (On the Field, With Infielders at Positions)—12 swings and then baserunning

From D. Keller, 2011, *Survival Guide for Coaching Youth Baseball* (Champaign, IL: Human Kinetics).

Focus on the Feet First

You may have to bite your tongue when you see certain flaws in your athletes' swings. Simply put, an athlete is *not* ready to receive that instruction or put it into practice effectively until the feet are fixed. It's like teaching long division before addition (as if any of us remember how to teach long division). Focus on the feet first and work from the ground up. Later, with proper balance and the ability to control the body, an athlete is more likely to take instruction on his swing and put it into use.

Squish the Bug and Hold the Finish

Power comes from the rotation of the trunk (hips and torso). Be patient and diligent in requiring athletes to rotate their back leg. This movement is referred to as squishing the bug. Turning the back leg fires the hips and starts the swing. This generates torque and drastically increases bat speed and power.

After you've had the chance to introduce the four positions of the swing, you should force a finish. Most athletes will slowly topple and will giggle and laugh as they lose their balance. If you can keep the challenge positive, but not quite a laughing matter, you can create an atmosphere where the hitter wants to hold a finish. At the conclusion of the swing, the hands should be high, and the back foot should be turned in. Make sure your description of squishing that darn bug is vivid and memorable. Then, have the athlete hold this position and look at it! When an athlete holds the finish, allows a coach to correct it, and looks at his body position, the athlete learns to feel the proper finish and begins to repeat it. This is commonly referred to as muscle memory.

No Fear

Having no fear applies to two areas with regard to hitting. First and foremost, an athlete cannot be afraid to swing and miss! Work hard to create an atmosphere where athletes are free from fear of failure. You do not want to celebrate swinging and missing, but as long as there is genuine effort, you cannot scold the athlete for missing the ball.

Second, work hard to eliminate the athletes' fear of getting hit. Drill 2 in this chapter directly addresses this fear, which is common among athletes seeing live pitching for the first time. Simply put, you must get the athlete to think *swing* first and *don't get hit* second. Many athletes have already allowed the latter into their mind when stepping into the batter's box. In theory, the fact that a coach may be pitching is supposed to help. But in reality, the rate of hit batsmen for coaches is comparable to that of a first-year pitcher.

Here is the thought process for an athlete who is thinking **swing** first and "get out of the way" second: *Swing, swing, swing—oh crap!* (as he gets hit by the ball). Here is the thought process for an athlete who is thinking **don't get hit** first and then trying to swing: *Oh crap, oh crap, oh crap—swing!* (as he swings late and misses the ball).

An athlete must think swing first and be surprised by a ball coming at him. If an athlete is focused on getting hit, he will take a defensive, weak swing. This is something that needs to be practiced. You should use controlled drills to build the athlete's trust that he will not be hit; over time, you can gradually move farther away and to a position where you are throwing at him. And if an athlete is scared of the baseball as it sits on a tee, consult a professional!

Back Elbow Up?

For generations and generations, fathers have told their sons to keep their back elbow up when hitting. By pointing the back elbow out, this seemingly meant the hitter was ready for action.

We believe that the reason this advice became popular was because people thought it helped keep the hitter's back shoulder from dropping.

Relax on this one, because sticking that elbow out too high can actually complicate the swing. Technically speaking, the first thing that the back elbow does when beginning the swing is quickly slot next to the body. Or, in other words, it drops! If the back elbow is way up and then the first thing it does is drop to the body, this can create a long, looping swing. Allow the athlete to position the back elbow where it's comfortable—just make sure that the back shoulder doesn't drop.

Bat Length and Weight

Babe Ruth has nothing on some of these kids! Ruth famously swung a 50-ounce bat—something difficult to imagine when you watch today's big leaguers swinging a 31- to 36-ounce variation. Many kids do their best to mimic the Great Bambino by using a bat better suited to a player twice their size. Two easy tests can be used to determine the appropriate length and weight of the bat for a particular player:

- **Length.** To test if the length of a bat is appropriate, stand the bat up on its cap. The handle of the bat should approach the athlete's waist or belt. Remember, this is where a belt *should* be worn, not necessarily where the belt is actually worn.

- **Weight.** To test if a bat is too heavy, have the athlete grab the bat with his dominant hand. Keeping the palm facing down, the athlete should try to hold his arm and the bat straight out in front of the body. With the athlete's arm fully extended, look to see if the athlete is strong enough to keep the bat pointing straight away (without letting it fall toward the ground) for 10 seconds. If the athlete can keep the bat pointing away from the body, chances are he's strong enough to swing it.

Bunting

For baseball players at the youngest ages, the most impressive bunts are often made with a full swing. But believe it or not, this is not by design. No, swinging bunts are typically the result of a hitter's helmet falling over the eyes, or a bat that weighs in about equal to the hitter's own body. But if your athletes are in kid-pitch, here are the beginning basics to teach about bunting:

- **Spin on the back foot.** The bunter should squish the bug—rotate the back foot and bend at the knees. The legs will move the body up and down, but the bunter should not square up or he'll get blasted in the chest. Keeping the foot in a straight-line position toward the pitcher gives the bunter the opportunity to turn and protect vital organs in case of a misdirected pitch.

- **Bend the knees to go up and down.** The bunter should try to use the knees as hydraulic lifts to raise and lower the body along with the bat. Moving the arms and hands is simply too difficult, and using the legs keeps the head in a good position to see the baseball.

- **Use a turtle bite with the top hand.** The top hand moves up to the middle of the bat, just below the base of the barrel. The bunter should grip the bat firmly between the thumb and inside of the index finger (figure 7.6). Referred to as a *turtle bite* in backyard wrestling matches, this grip helps to keep the fingers from getting smashed

Figure 7.6 Bunting grip and movement.

on an inside pitch. Basically, the fingers of the top hand should never reach onto the side of the bat facing the pitcher. The bunter should turtle bite that bat and save the fingers from being bitten by the baseball!

• **Slide the bottom hand up the bat.** In an effort to get better bat control, the bunter also slides the bottom hand up the bat, to a position somewhere near the top of the grip tape.

• **Keep the barrel up.** To keep the ball on the ground, the bunter should keep the barrel above the handle while in the bunting position. This means the top hand stays above the bottom hand, and the legs move the body down if the pitch is lower. This only comes into play if the unwritten rule of "make contact with the baseball" is being followed.

Coach's Note

Teach bunting by walking through the stance without any live baseballs. When involving live baseballs, get the athlete into bunting position before tossing anything. Once in that position, the athlete should work on holding the proper form while making soft contact with the baseball. After an athlete is able to make consistent contact, you can then move on to bunting drills with the athlete starting in a normal batting stance.

Baserunning

Baserunning is a series of sharp left turns! That may be a bit simplistic, but the basics of baserunning do rely on making lots of left turns. Quick-and-dirty Baserunning 101 centers on teaching two main fundamentals: running from home to first and running on a base hit.

Home to First Base

Also known as the hard 90, this is when a batter must run through the base in an effort to beat an infielder's throw. With a full-size diamond, the bases are 90 feet apart, which brings to life the term *hard 90*. At the youngest ages, the bases are set at 50 to 60 feet, but the fundamentals remain the same—run hard and hit the base! When teaching athletes to run from home to first, you need to communicate three main keys:

• **Step on the front half of the base.** Contrary to what the kids hear in school, they will be happy to learn that this in fact *is* a race. The goal is to touch the part of the base that is closest to the runner before the first baseman catches the ball. So the runner should step on the front half of that base.

- **Hit the base with either foot—don't miss the base!** This sounds funny, but it's an absolute must to clearly communicate this rule. It actually doesn't matter which foot the runner uses to step on first base with. Just try to explain the idea of hitting the base without breaking stride, and put most of your emphasis on stepping on the base. If this means the left foot, then the runner should use the left foot. Did I mention that the goal is to step on the base?

- **Break down afterward.** The phrase *break down* means to slow down, chop the steps, and come to a stop in an athletic stance. Older base runners will be taught to break down and look over their right shoulder. What are they looking for? If you said "overthrows," give yourself a treat and a pat on the back—you are really growing as a baseball coach. Of course, breaking down is always done several steps after the base . . . after stepping on the base . . . after stepping on the front half of the base . . . after stepping on the front half of the base with either foot. The emphasis here is on stepping on bases.

Base Hit

Here comes the banana! And this is a situation where those small plastic cones will be worth their weight in gold. The situation here is a clean base hit to the outfield. This is a time when the base runner *knows* he will at least have a single, potentially a double, and on certain occasions, a raucous round-tripper through multiple stop signs and plumes of brick dust smoke (cue the Benny Hill music, "Yakety Sax"). The basic idea is to touch first base, take a turn (the aforementioned left turn), and think about continuing on to second base.

- **Take a banana curve.** A sense of urgency is a good thing while running the bases. In certain cases, this will actually need to be taught. And in many cases, a sense of urgency will bring with it some degree of speed—pure, natural, blinding speed we hope! Running with speed means that there will be a rounded turn when approaching each base. It's impossible to make a 90-degree turn while running fast. And this absolutely, fundamentally needs to be taught.

The banana curve is the curved path taken 20 feet (6 m) before the base until 20 feet after the base. Place cones down starting on the baseline 20 feet before the base. Gently swing your cone line out 5 to 6 feet (1.5 to 2.0 cm) as you arch your banana curve; then bring the next couple cones back toward the base. Be sure to continue your curve beyond the base in order to show the base runners how to aggressively "take a turn" and look toward second base. It's now decision time regarding whether or not the runner will go for second. Aggressive mistakes should be encouraged when your players are running the bases. It's not as if they're going to listen to you anyway!

• **Hit the inside corner of the base.** The base may be flat, or the base may be raised. Either way, base runners should be taught to step on the inside corner of the base. You can continue your Baserunning 101 by clearly stating this: *Don't miss the base.* That said, point out that stepping on the inside corner of a raised base actually gives the runner something to push off of and the ability to lean into the turn slightly.

A great way to teach this is to stand on top of first base like a duck. Connect your heels at the far corner so that you cover most of the base and leave only the inside corner open for stepping on (see figure 7.7). This may set you up to get stomped on, but it's all in the name of coaching!

• **Use either foot—don't break stride!** Base runners should hit the inside corner of the bag, take an aggressive turn, and look to the ball in the outfield. At that point, they may need to reverse their turn and get back to the base pronto.

Figure 7.7 Cone banana curve with a coach standing on first base to expose the inside corner.

Drill 1 Three-Step Hitting

⚾BEGINNER

EQUIPMENT   Baseballs, bat

PURPOSE   This drill teaches the athletes to correctly position their feet at the stance position and then to properly take a short stride. When teaching hitting, you should begin with the feet, and this drill focuses on the importance of staying balanced while swinging. The athletes should swing hard and should not fall down! It's unbelievable how good of a coach you will be when none of your athletes fall over after swinging. And it's awesome to watch a youngster improve when given the basic fundamentals of a stance, stride, and finish.

PROCEDURE   Place three baseballs (or cones or markers of some sort) directly in front of the athlete's feet. These baseballs will mark the **only** three positions where the feet are allowed to be:

- **Ball 1:** Back-foot marker at setup or stance position
- **Ball 2:** Front-foot marker at setup or stance position
- **Ball 3:** Front-foot marker at stride or load position

Starting in the stance position, the athlete will place his feet directly behind the back two baseballs. The space between these baseballs (or markers) should be adjusted so that the balls are positioned just outside the athlete's shoulders. The front baseball should be placed 4 to 6 inches (10 to 15 cm) in front—at a position where the athlete would comfortably take a small stride or step.

To begin, the athlete steps into the stance and assumes the foot positioning behind the first two baseballs. Hitting a ball off of a tee (or from a coach's soft toss), the athlete should focus on taking a stride, taking a big swing, and then holding the finish. It's as simple as this: Challenge the kid to take a small step, swing, and *not* fall over. Sounds simple, but it's not! Limit the foot movement to a single stride, and instruct the athlete to hold the finish.

VARIATION *Broken swinging.* Incorporate freezes at stance, stride, and finish. First, have the athlete assume the stance position. On a coach's verbal command of "load," the hitter should take a short step to the first marker and also move the hands slightly back away from the body. With the athlete in this loaded hitting position, he should understand that the feet are set and will not move again! From here, you either toss the baseball up or simply issue the verbal command "explode," and the athlete takes his swing. Provided the athlete can hold his finish without moving the feet during the swing, you are quickly becoming an all-star coach!

COACHING POINTS *Focus on the feet.* Be careful not to try to correct too much with the athlete's swing or head movement, unless it pertains directly to what is going on with his feet. This drill is designed to firm up the athlete's foundation—his feet! With a solid foundation in place, the athlete can continue to build upward and develop a great swing.

Drill 2 Tee Work With Stance and Grip

EQUIPMENT   Batting tee, bucket of baseballs, bat

PURPOSE   In this drill, the athlete uses a stationary tee to learn the proper grip, stance, and footwork in addition to taking swings. All instruction assumes a right-handed batter.

PROCEDURE   Set up a tee with or without a catch net, and have the athlete stand next to the tee.

Step 1—find the proper stance. Remember that the athlete should make contact with the baseball just inside the front foot (after it strides forward). When taking a stance in front of home plate (or a tee with a home plate attached), athletes can follow a three-step process to find the proper positioning of the feet:

1. Touch the right toe to the closest corner of home plate (see photo *a*).
2. Place the left foot directly behind the right foot (touch the toe of the left foot to the heel of the right foot) (see photo *b*).
3. Step back with the right foot a distance just outside the width of your shoulders. At this point, the athlete should be balanced and comfortable with the knees slightly bent (see photo *c*).

Step 2—find the proper grip. Use another simple process to teach the position of the hands on the bat (descriptions are for a right-handed batter):

1. Extend the top arm (left hand) out over the plate. Keep the hand open with the palm facing down.
2. Extend the bottom arm (right hand) out over the plate. Keep the hand open with the palm facing up. Place the bottom hand right next to the top hand and keep the thumb pointing out (photo *a*).
3. Close both hands, trying to keep the palm-up, palm-down hand positioning (photo *b*).
4. Rotate the hands so that the right thumb now points directly up (photo *c*).
5. Move the hands to a position in front of the back shoulder (photo *d*).

(continued)

Step 3—use tee work to introduce grip, stance, and swing.

Use the tee station to allow athletes to get lots of good swings in a short amount of time. Place the ball on the tee and take advantage of the fact that the ball is not moving. Have the athlete focus on stance first, grip second, and then swinging the bat and hitting the ball. You can position the tee and baseball in different positions to challenge the hitter to find the barrel of the bat. With tee work, you can get as technical as you want. Depending on where you are at in the teaching process, you may involve any combination of stance, stride and load, and finish execution. If looking for swing repetitions, fire through repetitions of five to seven swings per athlete.

VARIATION *Inside and outside pitches.* For more advanced hitting training, position the baseball for an inside pitch or an outside pitch. Don't worry about how the athlete does it; just tell him to hit the baseball without changing the position of the feet. This means that the hands and swing will have to naturally adjust to hit the baseball with the barrel of the bat. And this moves the athletes toward advanced hitting technique!

COACHING POINTS *Truly teach.* This drill is an opportunity to truly teach the batting stance and grip. Take the time to explain and show the athlete where his feet end up relative to home plate and the pitcher. Often times, athletes get so preoccupied with swinging at the ball that they forget to take a look at home plate and see where they are standing. The footwork keywords of "right, left, right" can help a lot. Let them be the answer to a quiz after practice for a piece of candy!

Drill 3 Getting Hit

EQUIPMENT   Tennis or Wiffle balls, bat (for the athlete), glove (for the coach)

PURPOSE   This drill helps alleviate the fear of getting hit by a baseball by teaching the batter how to get hit properly. The drill is appropriate for all athletes stepping up to a coach-pitch division and for any athlete who is afraid of getting hit.

PROCEDURE   First, athletes should know that the fear of getting hit is one of the most common baseball fears around. Everyone is scared of getting hit; the key is to control that fear and *not* let it affect you as a hitter. The first part of this drill involves teaching the fundamentals of getting hit by a baseball. Yep, there's even a fundamentally sound way to get hit!

- The body should turn in to protect the vital body parts (see the photo). The back and front shoulder turn in toward the plate so that the rear of the front shoulder, the back, or the butt will receive the blow. Tell the kids that it might sting, but it's better to experience a sting than to break something.

- The bat head should drop beside the body. In addition to turning in, the athlete should drop the bat beside the body to eliminate any foul balls off the bat.

(continued)

Begin the drill by lightly tossing Wiffle balls or tennis balls directly at the batter. To protect against any unwanted confrontations, you may want to let another parent toss balls at your own son. A big part of this drill is the mental state of the athlete. At the start, let the athlete know that the ball *will* be thrown directly at him. Don't throw it hard, but do throw it at him and allow him to practice turning in and taking a "beanball." Remember, the batter expects to be hit, so let him have it!

VARIATIONS

1. *Swings added.* To help simulate getting hit in a game, have the athlete alternate between getting hit and taking a swing. Remembering the mental state of the athletes, start by clearly communicating when to swing and when to get hit. And follow the plan.

2. *Random swings.* Toss pitches primarily for strikes and mix in balls directly at the batter. The key here is to keep an athlete focused on taking the swing—not on getting hit. The athlete should be surprised and react to a ball directly at him: *Swing . . . swing . . . oh crap—turn in!* The athlete should turn in and protect his body as a defense mechanism, without losing that aggressive swing.

COACHING POINTS   *Make it fun.* This can be an intimidating drill, so keep it fun. Strike a deal with the batters that for every tennis ball that they get hit by (correctly), they can, in turn, pick up the ball and throw it back at you. Now, you stand tall and proud and take that tennis ball correctly—turn in and drop the bat!

Drill 4 Darts or Short Toss

EQUIPMENT One bucket of baseballs, Wiffle balls, or tennis balls; protective screen (to protect the coach)

PURPOSE This drill introduces live pitching; the ball is now coming from in front of the batter. In this drill, it's easy to throw strikes, allowing batters to get a large number of swings in a short time. If Wiffle balls are used, cleanup time is also minimized because the flight of the batted balls is cut down significantly.

PROCEDURE Set up a net 10 to 15 feet (3 to 4.5 m) in front of the batter and toss balls into the strike zone for swings. Sit on a bucket or chair, and be sure to get behind a protective screen or barrier (see the figure). If using Wiffle balls or Wiffle golf balls, you can get away with not using a screen, but even those things can sting when struck hard.

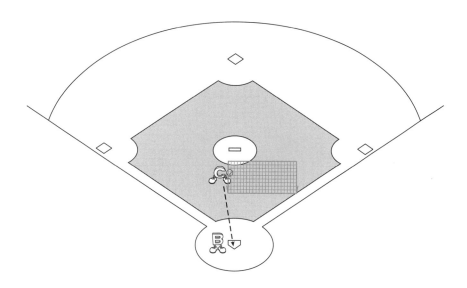

Sitting so close to the batter allows you to throw strikes. It's remarkably difficult to throw strikes to a four-foot human, especially when you have to control the trajectory of your throw to find the athlete's bat! Sitting on a bucket brings the ball down to the batter's height and allows you to simply reach back and toss the ball like a dart. More strikes mean more swings, and more swings mean shorter stations.

(continued)

VARIATION   *Wiffle ball rotation.* If Wiffle balls are used for this drill, athletes can rotate from hitter to fielder without the need for a glove. After taking 7 to 10 swings, the athlete should place his bat to the side of the drill area and move toward first base. The other athletes rotate around the infield to shag batted balls, eventually moving to an on-deck position and then to the position of live batter. Wiffle balls don't travel far, so the athletes can form a mini-infield 30 to 40 feet (9 to 12 m) away from the plate.

COACHING POINTS   *Get low, throw strikes.* Sitting close to the batter allows you to throw strikes consistently and also allows you to adjust your trajectory or speed to find the athlete's bat, which is one of the youth baseball coach's most difficult challenges! Now that you are 4-feet tall (although imposing, intimidating, and slightly overweight for a four footer), the ball comes from a more realistic height, and the batter can see it more easily. Remember, release the ego, throw strikes, and get the athlete swings.

Drill 5 Soft Toss With Details

EQUIPMENT Catch net, baseballs, Wiffle balls, golf-ball-size Wiffle balls

PURPOSE Soft toss is a controlled drill where the batted ball is caught by a net. Coaches can underhand toss the baseball (or Wiffle ball) into the strike zone from a short distance away. Unlike our high school hero trying to throw strikes from the mound, the coach uses this shortened toss to ensure accuracy and to introduce swinging the bat at a moving ball. The catch net collects batted balls, which eliminates time spent chasing baseballs.

PROCEDURE Soft toss can involve a number of variations. In a nutshell, the catch net is placed 5 to 7 feet (150 to 210 cm) in front of the batter. A coach sits or kneels directly to the side of the catch net, facing the batter, and tosses the ball lightly into the hitting zone (just inside the front foot at the stride position). Start by ensuring that the bat will remain in the batter's hands—instruct the batter to grip the bat firmly with two hands from the start of the swing until the end of it.

Designed to be used in a small space, the catch net stops the ball from flying. Heck, soft toss could be done in the backyard or inside the garage—not that you would ever bring baseball inside the house.

- **Baseballs and tee.** Use standard baseballs and place them on a tee. Start with a baseball that doesn't move, and aim to help the athlete experience hitting the ball hard.
- **Soft-tossed baseballs.** The coach soft-tosses baseballs, and athletes hit them into the net.
- **Wiffle balls.** Use Wiffle balls or golf-ball-size Wiffle balls to train eye–hand coordination.
- **One knee.** Have the athlete drop his back knee to the ground and extend his front leg toward the catch net. Taking swings from this one-knee position helps the athlete work on a proper swing path. You don't need to say much; just let the athletes swing and adjust. But you should provide instruction during a few practice swings to make sure no knees get whacked.
- **Two balls.** Toss two balls in the air and indicate which one the athlete should swing at. This can be very challenging, so have fun and use this variation only when appropriate.

(continued)

COACHING POINTS

1. *Add baserunning.* Most hitting drills done live on the field can involve some form of baserunning. After a set number of swings, have your athletes drop the bat and sprint to first base. Another coach or parent can help with baserunning details, introducing left turns around the bases. Be careful *not* to have athletes run home, however, because you do not want athletes to be in danger of being struck by a ball or bat.

2. *Add defense.* The same can hold true for adding defensive players or shaggers. Typically, hitting drills should be designed to minimize the number of athletes designated to shag duty. This is the perfect area to involve extra parents, brothers, or sisters. However, let's use the example of a 12-athlete team to see how defense could be added to batting practice. With 12 athletes broken into four groups, we have a maximum of 3 athletes per group. However, if group 3 is hitting live on the field, we need to pick up those baseballs and return them to the coach leading live batting. Place the defensive group (group 4) around the infield and have them work on fielding ground balls. Use the extra helpers (moms, dads, dogs) in the outfield to shag all other balls hit and to keep the drill moving.

   - **Group 1:** Instruction soft toss (foul territory behind the third-base dugout)
   - **Group 2:** Repetition Wiffle ball darts (bullpen area down the first-base line)
   - **Group 3:** Live hitting and tee work (on the main diamond)
   - **Group 4:** Defense during live hitting (on the main diamond)

The Coach's Clipboard

✔ Challenge your hitters to swing, hold a finish, and not fall over.

✔ Focus on the feet first. Use the Three-Step Hitting drill to simplify footwork.

✔ Design your batting practice to maximize swings by using small groups and multiple stations.

✔ Create the opportunity to teach by dedicating one station to instruction.

✔ Teach the stance, stride and load, and finish. This provides a basic plan that all athletes (and coaches) can follow.

✔ Help batters avoid the fear of being hit.

✔ Teach athletes the simple procedures for determining bat size, a proper stance, and a proper grip on the bat.

✔ Make sure your batters "squish the bug" in order to use the body and hit for power.

✔ Teach baserunning basics and find time in practice to introduce bunting.

✔ Use your help. Parents want nothing more than the therapy of chasing balls in the outfield.

On-Field Execution

Now that you're inching closer and closer to becoming a full-blown youth baseball coach, let's stop and take a look at how all of this information comes together on the field. Remember, all the knowledge in the world related to hitting or throwing a baseball isn't worth a bag of peanuts if you can't put it to use during practice. First, we'll cover some absolutes that each and every practice should contain. Then, we'll run through some tips and recommendations for handling common baseball-related occurrences.

Practice Absolutes

After a couple practices, you really will get the hang of it. You'll find that a natural rhythm begins to form, and you'll come to understand the ideal number of stations (and their time lengths) to be set up during a typical practice. As you progress through the season, you will need to consciously mix things up, adding fun, competition, and new drills to team workouts. Let's step back a bit and quickly review the core components of most practices.

Ingredients of a Baseball Practice

This is baseball, not rocket science. As a coach, once you understand the nuts and bolts of how stations work and how practices are structured—and then also establish a basic level of understanding of baseball skills such as hitting, throwing, and catching—you will see that a baseball practice is really nothing more than a simple six-step process. Here's a basic overview of a youth practice:

1. Run, stretch, and throw
2. Five Minutes for Fielding
3. Defensive stations
4. Offensive stations
5. Baserunning, conditioning, and agility
6. Team discussion or meeting

In addition, the following ingredients should be added regularly and randomly:

1. Fun
2. Competition
3. Novelty (something new)
4. Energy
5. Guest instructors

Let's finish with the following manager and coach responsibilities. Remember that you may—no, you *will*—fill both manager and coach roles.

1. Practice plan—manager
2. Field prep—manager and coach
3. Instruction—coach
4. Field cleanup—manager and coach
5. Updates and schedule—manager

You'll learn that there are lots of little tasks that can be assigned to athletes and their parents as well. Examples include pulling bases out of a shed, placing cones or baseball buckets in designated areas, and performing cleanup tasks. When a duo arrives early, put them to work! Raking fields, cleaning dugouts, and laying out equipment are things that both kids and parents *want* to be a part of. Much like a teacher, you should be firm early and delegate tasks aggressively—you'll be thankful later that you did!

Run, Stretch, and Throw   As described in chapter 2, each practice should start with some version of run, stretch, and then throw. At the Lifeletics Baseball Academy, the group jog has been supplemented with a relay competition on an ever changing obstacle course. Each morning, a staff architect designs the course, which is full of twists, jumps, barrel rolls, and bear crawls. Sprinkle in a handful of spins with the head down on a bat, and you've got yourself a really fun warm-up. Watch the kids laugh and scream, both for the humor involved and for the enjoyment of competition. This activity falls loosely under the category of *running,* but I can tell you from experience that this will kick off your practice with tons of energy and a team full of smiles!

Stretching is directly related to the age of your athletes. Select leaders and use this position of power as a reward for positive behavior or game performance. If a hitter hits a home run, you can make him a leader at the next practice. If a base runner goes back to the base on a pop fly, you can make him a leader. If a fielder catches a pop fly, you should drop to your knees and make sure that a parent caught it on video!

Sample Stretching Routine

Please note that these stretches are only suggestions. For a more thorough explanation or to identify the best combination of age-appropriate stretches, you should consult a physician or physical trainer. After some sort of active run, the kids should be panting; their heart rates will be pumping and their circulation flowing. For stretching, start with the legs and work from the ground up. Think of fun names for stretches, mix up the order, or involve verbal counting as a way to hold focus. Never underestimate the challenges associated with capturing 5 to 10 minutes of concentrated focus for stretching, especially when those doing the stretching can fold themselves in half with relative ease!

Lower body

Begin the lower body stretching with 10 to 20 jumping jacks. Because the kids just finished running, you want to make sure their legs are loose and that the kids are smiling.

- **Hamstrings:** Standing with legs straight and feet together, bend at the waist and hang down. Although you may feel significant tightness in your lower back or may feel a belt buckle digging into your belly, this stretch actually loosens and warms the hamstrings (the back of the upper thighs). After a 10-second hold, spread the legs and repeat the hang. Finish the hamstrings with 5 seconds in each direction—down to the left leg and down to the right leg.

- **Quadriceps:** Commonly referred to in kidspeak as the "flamingo stretch," this stretch works the front of the upper thigh—the quadriceps muscle. Grabbing one foot with a hand over the shoelaces, pull up and behind the body, as if trying to touch the bottom of the shoe to the hamstring or rear end. During this stretch, the knee should point down, and the pull on the foot should be gentle. Balance will be a big challenge because the athletes will be standing on one leg. Challenge the group early to see who can keep their balance the longest. If such a challenge is not issued, here is what will happen: One athlete will fall, all will laugh, and very soon thereafter, all athletes will suddenly lose their balance, thinking it is pretty funny to fall (guaranteed).

- **Groin:** This is called the butterfly stretch. Take a seat, connect the bottom of the shoes, and pull both feet in toward the groin area. The knees extending sideways become the butterfly wings. Grab the feet with both hands, place the elbows on the inside of the calf area, and gently push down to "spread the wings." This should force a deeper groin stretch. Hold for a count of 10 and then release. While the kids are doing the butterfly stretch, be careful not to encourage anyone to fly away. Once airborne, butterflies are difficult to catch.

- **Achilles and calf stretch:** From the ground, get up and onto all fours, as if doing a push-up (hands and feet touch the ground). With the feet close together, extend the bottom of one shoe toward the ground. Hold for a count of 10 and then switch legs. This stretches the back of the lower leg—the calf and Achilles.

Upper body

Begin with a series of arm circles. This helps to specifically fire the shoulder area and prepare the upper body for a full stretch.

- **Arm circles:** Swing the arms in circles (figure 8.1) to specifically warm up shoulder joints and muscles. Start small and work big—and remember, no flying away at any time.
  - 15 forward circles: 5 small, 5 medium, 5 big
  - 15 backward circles (turn palms up): 5 small, 5 medium, 5 big
- **Arm across body:** Point the right arm straight out in front of the body, parallel to the ground. Touch the opposite shoulder with the right hand. Grab the back of the right elbow and pull the arm across and slightly into the body. Straighten the arm to near full extension, and try to pull the elbow toward the shoulder (figure 8.2). Hold for a count of 10, and then repeat for the other arm.

- **Throwing arm behind head:** Point the right arm straight up toward the sky. Now, reach behind the head so that the hand is pointing down while the elbow is still pointing up toward the sky. Again, grab the back of the elbow of the right arm with the opposite hand. Gently pull the elbow behind the head (figure 8.3). To ensure the proper stretching angle, imagine bringing the right elbow in the direction of the left shoulder. Hold for a count of 10, and then repeat for the other arm.

Figure 8.1 Arm circles.

Figure 8.2 Arm across body.

Figure 8.3 Throwing arm behind head.

- **Forearm stretches** (hold each for a count of 10, and then repeat for the other arm):
  - **Fingers on top (stop sign stretch):** Extend the right hand straight out in front of the body, with the fingers pointing up to the sky (imagine telling someone to stop, showing the palm directly in front). Keeping the arm straight and parallel to the ground, use the opposite hand to gently pull the fingers back toward the body (figure 8.4). Be sure that the entire wrist stretches back toward the body. Many young athletes with loose joints will pull the fingers back and leave the wrist relatively straight.
  - **Fingers on bottom (Spiderman stretch):** Extend the throwing hand straight out in front of the body, with the palm facing the sky. Keeping the elbow straight and parallel to the ground, use the opposite hand to gently pull the fingers underneath the arm and toward the body (figure 8.5). Again, be sure that the entire hand is moving backward to stretch the forearm rather than the fingers.

Figure 8.4   Fingers on top.   **Figure 8.5**   Fingers on bottom.

- **Knuckles down (basketball shot follow-through):** Extend the throwing arm, with the fingers pointed to the ground; the palm faces the body, and the back of the hand faces away from the body. With the other hand, gently pull the back of the hand (not the fingers) toward the body (figure 8.6).

Figure 8.6 Knuckles down.

- **Finish:** Wrap up stretching with a full-body shake, swinging the arms front to back, as if giving a self-hug.

Throwing can also be widely defined depending on age. Have fun watching the kids progress as they learn to throw and catch. Start with basic fundamentals and add one extra piece during each practice. When the time is right, use the Five-Step Throwing Routine drill (p. 78) covered in chapter 5 to establish a routine that the athletes can learn and follow.

Five Minutes for Fielding

The period in between stretching and field practice is a great opportunity to insert some basic skill training—something related to the hands and feet that doesn't require a field. For the youngest ages, this might involve basic receiving, such as the Thumbs Up, Pinkies Down drill (drill 1 in chapter 4, p. 52) or Four-Corners Receiving drill (drill 2 in chapter 4, p. 54). Later in the season or for more advanced kids, try the Box Drills (drill 3 in chapter 3, p. 38) or the Ground Ball–Quick Catch drill (drill 4 in chapter 3, p. 40). This practice really doesn't have to take much more than five minutes, although it can—there are no rules here! Typically, this Five Minutes for Fielding time involves basic receiving or throwing, or what we call "baseball athleticism." You're trying to teach coordination specific to baseball. Although this doesn't happen overnight, this part of practice can be used to improve basic baseball movements.

Note: This practice component can be done *off* of the baseball field. Keeping this in mind, a team could stretch, run, throw, and then participate in Five Minutes for Fielding all without the need for a field. If the league has assigned your squad a field from 4:30 to 5:30 p.m. on Tuesday, you could easily start your practice at 4:00 p.m. and do so off of the main field. By conducting the beginning portions of your practice before your official field time begins, you can save the dedicated time on the field for those drills that require the diamond. In reality, entire practices can be run effectively without a field. But when a field is made available, work hard to have your athletes ready to take advantage of this valuable time.

Defensive and Offensive Stations

Defensive and offensive stations are the nuts and bolts of your practice. This station instruction time is when you unleash the coach inside of you. A dynamite practice plan will allow all coaches to have the opportunity to teach. But even if a volunteer doesn't have the knowledge or ability to teach, you can put this person in a station dedicated to repetition—tossing batting practice, hitting ground balls, or shagging. Take good care of your help, and your help will take care of you. Cookies, thank-you cards, and beverages are often ample pay for volunteer coaches.

In general, you should conduct defensive stations before offensive stations. Kids love to hit! And they will always find the energy to swing the bat. If defense is covered before offense, you won't hear any complaints when it comes time to break out the bats. But if you tire the kids out with swings, batting practice, and offensive training—and then try to get the group to squat down and hold the fielding triangle position—you're in for a firestorm of complaints and whining.

And remember, at this age group you want to focus on fundamentals. Specific strategies and plays really apply mostly to older kids, and if taught at all, should be kept simple.

Baserunning   The architect of the obstacle course for the running segment of practice has another chance for glory! The main priority during the baserunning segment is to teach the kids to run the bases. But other goals include building stamina, increasing leg strength, and getting the gang in shape. All of this should be done while having fun. Obstacle courses, four-corner cone squares, and relay races can help keep smiles on the athletes' faces while they are working hard. It's a good idea to keep the pace of practice at a high enough level to keep the kids sweating (always being careful to allow breathers and water breaks); however, you should use the final 15 minutes of practice to teach base-running and kick in to high gear. Fight the video game and computer hours with consistent exercise at every practice.

Team Discussion or Meeting   Always conclude practice with a team meeting. Use this time to review upcoming schedules and events, to cover off-the-field issues, or to review team rules. Find a way to end each practice on a positive note, and point out several highlights of the day's events. Praise your athletes for giving effort—not necessarily for performance—and put special attention on those athletes who go for it. Because you want your team to play without fear of failure, you must find a way to point out and reward aggressive mistakes. Your athletes will have various ability levels, so the one consistent thing you can look for is effort. As long as the athletes are swinging aggressively, there's nothing wrong with a strikeout. And if a shortstop shows a good fielding triangle and shuffles his feet toward the first baseman—before airmailing a throw into the first row of parents—there is nothing wrong with throwing a ball away. Athletes must fail in order to truly learn from their mistakes. It's the head coach's job to keep all attitudes positive and to reward effort along the way.

Field Prep, Equipment, Execution, and Best Practices

Let's say practice starts at 4:00 p.m. You need to be there by 3:30 p.m., which means your boss may not like you during baseball season. On arrival, get your delegation on . . . even if only to your own kid! Litter the field with disc cones as close as possible to where they will be used during the first round of defensive stations. Don't forget side-by-side cones for each station and a couple by the stretching and throwing area to guide the lines and catch partners. Place baseball buckets at their appropriate places, put Wiffle balls in the other hitting areas, and spread out any other equipment to be used for practice that day.

Next, turn your focus onto the field itself. This means grabbing bases and any available screens or nets out of the equipment bin, and then giving some love to the infield dirt. If you plan on using the mound, a quick rake might be necessary for it as well. As kids begin to show up, one of the other volunteer coaches will also likely arrive. Have this coach take over the field prep duties or guide prepractice games and then stretching. If today's practice calls for an obstacle course, this can be something that an assistant coach sets up while monitoring prepractice games.

Prepractice Games Following the rule that athletes should first run and then stretch before throwing, there needs to be a 10- to 15-minute gap between the time when the early birds show up and when they begin throwing. The first thing every father will do after walking up with his son is start playing catch. And really, how can you blame him? Although it may be difficult, you'll need to explain the ideas behind throwing only after warming up and stretching first. Do this well and respectfully, then carefully manipulate that father into leading a group in a prepractice game. Prepractice games fill the gap between arrival and the start of stretching, and they are designed to keep athletes busy without throwing.

- **Flip.** The most common prepractice game involves a baseball-themed game of hot potato. With the group in a small circle, the athletes simply cannot let the ball touch the ground. They toss the ball around using the glove, without catching it or holding it for more than a second. Essentially, the goal is to redirect the ball or flip it to another player, which helps to train glove work and coordination. Most important, the game is really fun, and there's no throwing (other than picking up a dropped baseball and tossing it to get started again). Add competition by turning the player's hat after a drop. If a player drops the ball, his hat is turned one-fourth of the way around. After four drops, the hat has turned all the way around, and the player has a strike against him. Three strikes and he's out (or he just moves to another game of flip).

- **Two-ball.** Another small-circle game, this simple game involves trying to catch two balls at once. No gloves are required; the challenge is to catch two balls tossed your direction with both of your bare hands, at the same time. Encourage clean and fair play because these games can be dangerous if baseballs start flying at players aggressively. After you catch (or attempt to catch) the two balls, it is then your turn to toss. Keep the energy up and the attitudes positive, and see how many tosses your group can go without dropping a ball.

Punctuality
Lead by example on this one, practicing what you preach, but also make sure that you're vocal about preaching punctuality. Especially at the first couple team events, you should be sure to let the parents know the importance of starting on time. And if they're late, let them know! Be careful though; you want to make friends, not enemies.

Typically, tee-ballers are not driving yet, so it's the parent's responsibility to get them to practice on time. In high school, if a player is late to practice or doesn't show up, that player doesn't play. It's as simple as that. Now, this isn't high school, but you're doing everyone a favor by teaching a respect for punctuality when it comes to baseball. Start practice on time and with a whistle or verbal command to start stretching. This will help athletes realize the importance of being on time and not disrupting practice or standing out from the group by being late. Any late athletes must run and stretch on their own before joining the workout.

Attire
At Lifeletics, the motto is "Dress like a champion, play like a champion." Shirts are tucked in, and hats are straight. The importance of this rule (and other rules) is relative to the age of the athletes. Athletes should wear a hat, cleats, baseball pants, and protective cup. And they should bring with them a bag of some sort containing their baseball glove and a bat and helmet if they have them. A little discipline goes a long way; athletes really do want structure, and they need discipline—firm first, relaxed second.

Communication   Clearly communicate policies on playing time, punctuality, discipline, and practice or game-day itineraries. Doing this early in the season prevents issues later and establishes an atmosphere of respect and efficiency. For your team to remain drama free, you must communicate clearly. At each practice, bring the team together before stretching or after throwing to quickly review the day's events, drills, and goals. And remember to finish with team time as well.

Consistency   If you want to avoid the headaches and hassles of politics, you need to be consistent with all team rules, policies, and disciplines. Treat all athletes and parents the same while keeping the big picture in mind at all times—you are coaching a Little League team, not a small unit in the military or a professional baseball team. Playing time should be equal among young athletes, and positions should be rotated regularly.

Combining Pieces   The ideas covered in chapter 2 on station instruction and time blocks are designed to maximize the time coaches spend teaching and athletes spend playing. Combining pieces can help to accomplish multiple goals. For example, you can combine baserunning with conditioning to make sure that athletes learn baserunning technique while also getting a cardiovascular workout. Or you can include a live defense station during batting practice where fielders work on fielding and throwing to first or second base.

Distractions   The amount and severity of team distractions will be directly linked to your skills as a practice planner. A loosely planned practice with athletes continually standing in long lines will lead to distractions such as digging holes, throwing rocks, pushing, and shoving. You can use the techniques described throughout this book to help keep distractions to a minimum; however, you should be aware that each group of kids will inevitably have one or two athletes who feel the need to show everyone the caterpillar they just found or a sweet somersault or head spin. The best strategy for disciplinary action is to pull the athlete out of the spotlight and the attention of others. Do not raise your voice, and do not allow yourself to get angry. Instead, move the athlete away from the drill or activity and have him sit right next to you. Do not stop working with the rest of the kids—that way, the distracting athlete is forced to sit and watch. With the spotlight off of the distracting athlete, his desire to be part of the team will soon overtake his desire to be on stage. After three or four minutes, you should calmly ask the athlete if he is ready to return to the group and work with the team. Allow the athlete to join the group, and encourage the other players to greet him with high fives. Then, quickly get the action going once again so that the focus stays on the team and the activity.

If the athlete causes a second distraction in a short amount of time, you should impose a penalty before pulling the athlete aside. For example, have the athlete run and touch the fence or a tree and then come back to you. Unless, of course, the caterpillar really is *that* cool. In this case, show the entire group the caterpillar, set said caterpillar free, and get back to work. After a second distraction, explain somewhat more firmly that this behavior will not be tolerated, and then return your focus and attention to the group. Be careful not to send a disruptive athlete to the dugout. The dugout contains a lot of equipment and other things that the athlete can use to keep himself occupied. Instead, keep that athlete very close to you so you can control the lack of attention.

Side-by-Side Cones

Side-by-side cones are a perfect follow-up topic to the discussion about distractions. You should use side-by-side cones to help athletes pay attention. Place two cones off to the side of each training area; the cones should be placed 20 to 30 feet (6 to 9 m) apart from each other. Use these cones as anchors for athletes to line up in between. The athletes should be parallel to one another, an arm's distance apart (side by side), in between the cones. This places the kids in a horizontal line, facing you, and it really helps to minimize distractions. The athletes are physically unable to grab or poke each other, and you can easily see all the athletes. Side-by-side cones should be a part of every station on the field and should be a regular part of the rotation routine. When a group arrives at a station, they can put their equipment in a pile or against a fence and immediately find the side-by-side cones. This shortens the amount of time wasted in between stations and increases the time you spend coaching.

At the first practice, you will need to provide some guidance on how to line up in between the cones, but soon the team will not even require a reminder. Knowing that it's time to listen, the kids will hustle to get into formation, and learning can begin. Distractions are much more difficult for the kids to create when all hands and feet can be seen by the coach and when there is nothing to hide behind.

Cones   Use cones or physical guides to mark the field—and use a lot of them! When you have limited field space and time, cones can serve as quick points of reference, can guide movements, and can greatly assist with keeping execution areas free of wandering athletes. Kids crave structure, and the proper use of simple disc cones can be an amazing help!

Firm First

Begin early-season practices with a heavy hand and a disciplined, no-nonsense environment. As with teaching, it's much more difficult to bring back an unruly classroom than it is to let a disciplined group relax. Start with a tough-love approach in order to establish an efficient team structure and to teach the kids to enjoy accomplishing goals and improving. Then, be sure to make practice fun and enjoyable. You can teach athletes to have fun while working out!

The Coach's Clipboard

✔ Follow the six practice absolutes to keep practices fun and exciting.

✔ Delegate early and treat your help well.

✔ Communicate consistently, including holding team discussions before and after practice.

✔ Use prepractice games to keep kids entertained before stretching.

✔ Create an obstacle course as a fun way to warm up before practice begins.

✔ Use side-by-side cones to help keep the coaches coaching and the players playing during practice.

✔ Handle distractions quickly and calmly without losing your temper.

✔ Be a firm leader first and the cool coach later.

✔ Litter the field with equipment and as many cones as possible.

✔ Laugh, smile, and have fun!

Game Day! What's My Role Again?

It's finally time to play ball. Game day is here, and your athlete has a bright, clean uniform on. So what if it's 6:30 a.m.? The game doesn't start for seven hours, and your little slugger is tugging on the sheets to get you out of bed. *This* is what you signed up for. It's time to let the kids play; time to see how far they've come; time for smiles, cheers, frowns, and tears—it's game day, baby!

Pregame routines are always subject to change. With the added energy and excitement of crowded parking lots and freshly stocked snack bars, it's not difficult to understand why kids might have trouble staying focused on why they are actually at the park. They may not be interested in stretching, warming up, or doing pregame drills, but that is your challenge as a coach—the reason why *you* are at the park: Your job is to keep the kids on task with smiles on their faces. At the end of the day, the kids are at the park to learn the game of baseball, learn valuable lessons from competition, and have lots and lots of fun. Edit and adjust as you learn what works for your team. And always be sure to enjoy the day!

Game-Day Plans

Two documents are extremely helpful in guiding the game-day activities. The first document, the Game-Day Coaching Plan, lists the day's schedule and helps to align coaches with their responsibilities. The second document, the Batting Lineup and Positions Sheet, is an overall snapshot of the game's innings, positions played, and lineup order. You can use these two documents to answer many of the kids' questions, such as "Where am I playing?" and "When am I hitting?" You're on your own for the always-tough "What's for snack today?"

Game-Day Coaching Plan

This document (see figure 2.3, p. 19) lays out the day's schedule and all that needs to be handled. Although this document primarily helps coaches with their roles, we've found that it is also useful for keeping players (and their parents) informed about what they are expected to do and when they are expected to do it. The document can be helpful for you as well. For example, on more than one occasion, I've been reminded by an athlete that our starting pitcher needs to go warm up: "Isn't it time for Johnny to warm up?" he asks. The trick here is to quickly act as if you were just about to do that, or you can look frantically around for that mythical coach whom you had asked to warm Johnny up. Then, get your glove and head to the bullpen pronto.

Batting Lineup and Positions

Post this lineup document (figure 9.1) right next to the Game-Day Coaching Plan so that athletes can be prepared to hit in the correct order and to take the field in the correct positions. This simple grid lists the athletes in the left-hand column, in the order of the batting lineup. The inning numbers are listed across the top, and the columns under these numbers indicate each player's position for that specific inning. Taking the time to map out the game's positions helps ensure that all league rules with regard to playing time are followed and that athletes are getting ample innings at various positions. Doing this "on the fly" is much more difficult than it may seem, especially with the recent addition of rules to protect young arms (e.g., athletes having just pitched are not able to play catcher). Having this mapped out in advance not only helps you to avoid issues with playing time and positions played, but it also empowers athletes to read the lineup and know which position they are playing.

Figure 9.1   Sample Batting Lineup and Positions Sheet

Order	#	Player	Position					
			Inning 1	Inning 2	Inning 3	Inning 4	Inning 5	Inning 6
1								
2								
3								
4								
6								
7								
8								
9								
10								
11								
12								

From D. Keller, 2011, *Survival Guide for Coaching Youth Baseball* (Champaign, IL: Human Kinetics).

Game-Day Schedule

For coaches, game day means that the fields must be prepped and the players must be prepared. Your responsibilities are most heavily weighed before the first pitch is thrown. And the simple structure established during your practices carries over well to game days. The following is a typical schedule for game days:

1. Pregame responsibilities
2. Run, stretch, and throw
3. Team time
4. Pregame warm-up
5. Pitcher warm-up and team sprints
6. Game time
7. Postgame

Pregame Responsibilities

Because there's a game to play, the foul lines and batter's boxes need to be chalked, the mound needs to be prepped, and the infield dirt needs to be raked or dragged. Your team will need an official scorekeeper, someone to count the pitches, and a rotating family responsible for snacks (put the team mom in charge of organizing snacks). NEVER forget the snacks! And keep an extra supply of nonperishable snacks in your car just in case that does happen. Be sure to review chapter 1 and bring with you your gear bag, team equipment, and athlete binder. Dot your i's and cross your t's at home, so that once you reach that field you can dedicate your focus to the game and those wonderful kids.

Run, Stretch, and Throw
Use the team warm-up time to make sure that the fields are game ready, that umpires have been assigned to your game, and that you have the necessary game balls for play. With the help of an assistant coach, the players should get loose with some sort of run, a thorough stretch, and a game of controlled catch. A good time to start the run, stretch, throw sequence is one hour before game time. Even though the field may not be available, you can begin the team's jog and stretching off of the playing field.

Team Time
This part of game day is extremely broad in definition. Use team time to hit players ground balls and fly balls, to take batting practice, or to go over signs and dugout etiquette. Review specific team goals, and make sure that all players have the chance to communicate important facts before the game begins—such as what they ate, who slept over last night, and where they will be going after the game.

Pregame Warm-Up
Teams with players who have reached age 9 or 10 will usually take what is called pregame infield and outfield. This is a scripted routine of defensive plays moving from position to position, intended both to warm up athletes and to remind them of simple fundamentals. Although there are no rules specifying what must be covered in a pregame routine, most coaches start with a series of ground balls and fly balls to the outfield positions before moving to the infield. Outfielders at each position are hit balls that they must throw to second base, third base, and then home plate. Involve infielders and work on cuts and relays with the right positions serving their relay responsibilities. Next, bring the outfielders in and work around the infield positions. Hit ground balls and

instruct athletes to make throws to first, second, and home plate. Add a twist here and a fun play there, keep the energy high, and get the kids ready to play.

Pitcher Warm-Up and Team Sprints

After the warm-up is done and the field has been cleared, it's time for the starting pitcher to get loose. Skip this step if playing tee ball or coach-pitch, unless your designated parent pitcher needs to work through game-day jitters. A coach can start warming the pitcher up, but bring in the starting catcher as soon as possible. Have the pitcher warm up his arm and work through any specific drills or rituals that have proven successful. Limit the pitch count to 15 to 25; this ensures that the starter is well warm but not worn out. The rest of the team can walk down the outfield foul line and run four to six warm-up sprints. If the players are old enough to lead off and steal bases, another coach can act as pitcher and simulate pickoff moves and pitches to home plate. Players like this short ritual because they often see it when they go to the big-league park. In fact, you should be sure to point out the similarity between their routine and those of the major leaguers.

Game Time—In-Game Responsibilities

Many moving parts come into play once the first ball is hit. To keep stress levels low, you need to leverage your assistant coaches well. The Game-Day Coaching Plan and the Batting Lineup and Positions Sheet should be clearly posted in the dugout. Here are some roles that need to be filled during the game:

• **Third-base coach.** The offensive guru typically coaches third base! An intense and demanding role, the third-base coach makes high-pressure decisions regarding when to bunt, steal, or hit-and-run. And with players at the youngest levels, this same guru places the ball on the tee, assists base runners in finding the next base, and consoles those who have been called out. The true role of the third-base coach is as head cheerleader, ensuring that batters swing hard and leave the field with a smile on their face.

• **First-base coach.** The first-base coach may be a player or parent depending on league guidelines. If this role is filled by a parent, this person will assist base runners with details once they are at first base. The first-base coach must be ready to help base runners find first base and decide when to run for second.

- **Dugout monitor.** A coach must be assigned to monitor the dugout and the unavoidable chaos contained within that small cage. Equipment should be kept neat and organized; player bags should be tucked underneath a bench or clipped to the fence. Kids will be kids. They will burp and blow bubbles, laugh and scream, but a dugout monitor should aim to keep this energy focused on the game itself. The games should be fun, but not to the point that player focus is taken away from the field of play and from teammates who may need the support of players in the dugout. Award a *Dugout Dude of the Day* for that athlete who best shows good sporting behavior and class—cheering on his buddies, picking up trash, and keeping his equipment neat and tidy.

- **Defensive architect.** Many athletes believe that playing defense is the perfect time to catch up on their gardening skills. This can include grass picking, dirt digging, and an observation of that day's cloud patterns. And although the importance of horticulture cannot be refuted, a defensive coach can help to keep athletes' focus on the game being played. This coach is responsible for reminding the players of the "20 eyes on the prize" rule. This team rule means that when a ball is placed live on the tee or a pitch is thrown, each and every defensive player has two eyes on the ball. Use this as a verbal reminder for defensive players to get into a ready position before each pitch. And yes, if you have 9 defenders, that would really only be 18 eyes. Whether in the dugout or actually in the field, the defensive architect shifts infielders accordingly for right-handed and left-handed batters, moves outfielders in or out, and issues friendly reminders of possible plays to be made in certain situations.

Postgame

The game has finished in victory or defeat, and your job now is to clear the dugout and wrap up the day. While parents prepare team snacks and clean up the seating area, you should collect team equipment and player bags as soon as possible and move the players and coaches into foul territory or behind the dugout for a team meeting. Wrap up the game on a positive note, review plays and players of the game, and cover any areas needing discussion. It's okay to point out areas that need to be worked on, but you should keep this time positive and be sure that each and every athlete leaves with a smile on his face. Use candy, baseball cards, or pizza certificates as prizes for outstanding play or good sporting behavior. Make sure that each player receives an award at some point during the season. Review the week ahead and the next team function, then finish with an earth-shaking team yell. You may want to get aggressive on this yell, because now you have to start thinking about getting caught up on those projects at work that are suffering from your early departures for baseball practice during the week!

Coaching Notes for Game Day

Follow these guidelines for an easy game day.

- **Playing time.** Put your ego aside and swallow your pride when filling out player positions. Work to fill out playing time equally across all players. As athletes grow older, the lineup will get more competitive. For beginning baseball players, however, playing time is something that should be evenly distributed—each athlete sits out for the same number of innings. Making the lineup and filling out positions are the most difficult part of game days. This is why the Batting Lineup and Positions Sheet should be filled out before leaving for the field on game days.

- **Positions.** Similar to playing time, positions played is another difficult puzzle to put together. There will be many times when your lineup on defense will *not* give you the best chance of winning. But you must stay strong and keep the big picture in mind. A rotating lineup will give players the opportunity to play multiple positions during the course of a game and over a season. Athletes should play both infield and outfield every game with the goal of developing baseball skills. Develop first, win second!

  Communicate these policies on playing time and positions played (as part of your coaching philosophy) to parents before competition begins. Parents love to win. It's human nature and brings out the best and worst in everybody. Parents will appreciate having a clear understanding of your coaching philosophy before an issue comes up during a game. If one of these decisions does end up resulting in an extra run or even a loss, you can simply point to the bigger picture and philosophy that was explained early in the season.

- **Signs**. As long as the competition at the tee ball level is within reason, signs won't be necessary. But when your players get to the win-at-all-cost age of 7, you best have a full arsenal of encrypted signs. Not really, two or three will do. Swipe an arm or hand across your chest to tell the batter or runner what play is on:
  - Bunt
  - Steal
  - Hit-and-run (base runner steals and batter must swing)

- **Umpires.** The umpires for your games will often be your fellow volunteer coaches—that is, volunteer coaches who are volunteering additional time as umpires. Treat them as you would like to be treated, and understand that they are doing their best in an unfamiliar role. If a rule is misinterpreted or incorrectly applied, call time-out and present your case. If a dispute arises over safe versus out, ball versus strike, or fair versus foul, remember that a judgment call is simply that—the umpire's judgment. A judgment call typically will not be reversed. A terrific rule presented by the Positive Coaching Alliance states this: The dugout should never hear a word you say to the umpires. This rule is a great way to help coaches keep their cool and always maintain a level head during games. Call time-out, approach your buddy behind the umpire's mask, and calmly tell him how much he stinks. Keep all bases securely fastened to their pegs, and always avoid hurling water jugs and bat racks.

- **Parents.** Make sure that parent comments are supportive and positive. Request that they do *not* make comments to the umpires and do *not* coach their kids from the stands. The kids are there to play, and parents should stay out of the way. Parents should leave the games to the players and coaches and then have a good talk after the game.

- **Big picture.** Athletes will have the biggest game of their lives each and every year—the 9-year-old's league playoff game, the 10-year-old's championship game, the 11-year-old's all-star tournament, and so on. Each season will present bigger and more pressure-packed situations. It is the job of parents, and specifically the head coach, to keep a level head and big-picture perspective of youth baseball during competition. Through your coaching, keep the focus on the development of these 12 kids—not on championships and trophies. The adults must think clearly while the kids think emotionally. Governing bodies such as PONY (Protect Our Nation's Youth) and Little League Baseball have put in place helpful rules such as pitch count and inning limitations to help protect young arms. Follow these rules and recognize the value of guidelines in helping to make tough decisions when under pressure to win.

The Coach's Clipboard

✔ Put your kid to bed with his uniform on—this saves at least 15 minutes of sleep in the morning.

✔ Use the Game-Day Coaching Plan to list the day's schedule and to outline responsibilities.

✔ Write up and post a Batting Lineup and Positions Sheet so that athletes know where to be.

✔ Assign each coach a pregame, postgame, and in-game job.

✔ Never, ever get caught without a snack. Keep an extra snack supply in the car!

✔ Award a Dugout Dude of the Day each game to that athlete who shows good sporting behavior and teamwork.

✔ Rotate positions from infield to outfield and make sure that batting lineups constantly change.

✔ Never allow a player or parent to overhear your discussion with an umpire.

✔ Encourage parents to stay positive, leave the umpires alone, and avoid coaching from the stands.

✔ Remember this: Practices are for coaches; games are for players. Keep this in mind and let the kids play!

Summary

Coaching youth baseball is a life-changing experience. It is an amazing opportunity to lead 12 athletes as they grind, compete, and grow together over a four-month season. The time spent with these youngsters will be challenging, frustrating, fulfilling, and unforgettable. Yes, winning is important, but teaching positive sporting behavior, the joys of competition, and character-building lessons trumps all!

If respected, this role as baseball coach will return tenfold the time, effort, and heart put into it. Structure, organization, and preparation are the keys to success. From the parent meeting to the stations during batting practice, if you take the time to plan out your manager responsibilities, the time spent as coach will truly involve teaching the game. A hearty high five to you for taking on this responsibility.

Picture this: Walking up to the will call window, you nervously tell the attendant your name. *I wonder if he remembered me,* you ask yourself as the attendant sifts through envelope after envelope unsuccessfully. *There are probably tons of people who he had to leave tickets for,* you think, *parents, friends, agent, sponsors.* Still, no luck. Then, the will call attendant pulls out the final envelope and looks up at your ragged baseball cap, sunglass tan, and six-pound bag of sunflower seeds. Calmly, she states, "This must be you." As she slides the envelope under the glass window, you look down curiously to see what might have caused the confusion—two front-row tickets stuffed inside an envelope with a single, unforgettable name written on the envelope: *Coach.*

Best of luck, Coach.

About the Author

Dan Keller is the president and owner of Lifeletics Sports Instruction in Huntington Beach, California. A lifelong student of the game of baseball, with a particular interest in pitching, he started Lifeletics in 2001 and has built it into a household brand providing world-class fundamental training with an emphasis on positive character development and the life lessons learned through athletics.

Keller experienced athletic success from youth baseball through the collegiate ranks and was drafted by the Baltimore Orioles in 1995. Since 2000 he has worked as a private pitching instructor for youth league and professional athletes. His team coaching resume includes work with competitive youth teams and teams at all levels of high school play.

Keller's work has been featured extensively in *Collegiate Baseball Newspaper*, *Junior Baseball Magazine*, and several online publications. He's also a frequent instructor for a number of youth clinics. In his free time he enjoys staying active by hiking and playing basketball, softball, and golf. Keller lives in California with his wife, Erin.